ESSE
FONTAI

2nd EDITION

"There is no place where the young are more gladly conscious of their youth, or the old better contented with their age."

R. L. Stevenson, *Fontainebleau*, 1882

Alasdair Crofton on the white circuit at Rocher Canon

ESSENTIAL FONTAINEBLEAU

2nd EDITION

Edited by

John Watson & Colin Lambton

STONE COUNTRY

Stone Country Press Ltd.
61 Sinclair Drive, Glasgow, G42 9PU, Scotland

Second edition

ISBN 9780992887605

A catalogue record for this book is available from the British Library

Design by Stone Country

www.stonecountry.co.uk

DISCLAIMER

The authors and publishers of this guide accept no responsibility for accident or injury incurred while using the guide. Remember, bouldering is an unroped climbing activity and requires care and attention at all times. The decision to climb is your own responsibility – be wise and look after each other!

ACKNOWLEDGEMENTS

Thanks are due to all who contributed to this guide and helped build a tribute to the forest:

Adrian Crofton
Arran Curran
Chris Everett
Chris Fryer
Chris Houston
Colin Lambton
Dan Varian >>> www.beastmaker.co.uk
Gareth Stott
John Coll
John Sharples
Lee Collier
Michael Jeans
Neil Richardson
Paul Roberts
Roddy MacKenzie
Sandra Spence
Sean Bell >>> www.seanbellphotography.com
Stewart Brown
Stuart Stronach
Sven Jonuscheit
Tim Morozzo >>> www.morozzo.co.uk
Victoria Taylor

CONTENTS

❐ Cuvier Rempart > Duroxmanie > © Sean Bell Photography

❒ France > Île de France

❒ Forest of Fontainebleau

Travel & Accommodation Notes

Most visitors to Fontainebleau either fly, drive or combine the two. The best airports to arrive at are of course near Paris: Beauvais, Charles de Gaulle and Orly. Travel time to the forest ranges from 1 to 2 hours from these airports. Make sure you bring a good Paris motorway map or rent a Sat-nav, you'll need it! To negotiate the intimidating motorways on your way south from the airports, travel east round Paris and find and stay on the N104 *La Francilienne* truckers' route, then follow signs for Lyon and the A6 *Autoroute du Soleil* – Fontainebleau will eventually appear on the road signs. Avoid being dragged into Paris and the nightmarish *Boulevard Périphérique* motorway ring-road, though this is usually an experience that happens only once!

By train: make your way to Gare du Lyon station in Paris, where regular trains run south to Fontainebleau via Melun in about 40 minutes. The local train line is *Transilien*, look out for terminal destination Montargis. Your arrival station is Fontainebleau-Avon and your ticket required is a 'Billet Ile-de-France à Fontainebleau–Avon'. To buy your ticket, go to the *Transilien Ile-de-France* ticket window or use the green ticket machines located in the main hall. Most trains depart from the lower Melun line 'RER' line down the escalators, follow the signs for the Melun platforms and go through the ticket gates. You can get off at Bois-le-Roi and walk into the forest (Rocher Canon being the nearest venue). There are no buses serving the forest so a car or bike is essential if you don't like walking!

It is not essential to have a car once you are in the forest, but it is useful for visiting areas outside the Trois Pignons and to get in and out of the towns for supplies. Whatever car you bring or hire, make sure you have adequate insurance, and leave no belongings in the car – it is wise to empty and open the glove compartment and remove the parcel shelf, showing nothing to give thieves an excuse. This is true in the campsites and outside gîtes as well. Diesel is known as 'Gazole' (usually black or yellow pumps). Make sure your car has plenty of fuel, oil and 'refroidissement' (coolant). Sat-nav is useful for the motorway connection from the airports. A useful road for navigating the forest is the circular 'Route Ronde'. The main towns you will need to get to know are Barbizon, Milly-la-Forêt, Le Vaudoué, L'Archant, Malesherbes and Nemours.

❐ *Check your route before you go*

The best idea is to arrange accommodation in advance, with many pre-booking a holiday house known as a 'gîte'. These can vary in capacity from around 2 to 8 people and are reasonably cheap in the 'off-season' (Oct-March), which is handy as these are the best months for climbing conditions. Visit *www.gites-de-france.com*. There is a good English-language climbers' gîte run by Neil and Chris Hart at Buthiers in the southern area: *www.maisonbleau.com* and a fine and friendly collection of chalets/B&B at Arbonne la Forêt: *www.gitearbonne.com*. Cheap hotels can be found in Fontainebleau and Nemours.

❐ *www.gitearbonne.com*

Wild camping is not allowed in the forest but the most convenient campsite is called *La Musardière*, in the Trois Pignons area just east of Milly-la-Forêt (on the Route des Grandes Vallées road, signed off the D409). This campsite is within walking distance of many good bouldering areas and is probably the best place to base yourself for a first-time visit, as you will meet other climbers and the facilities are excellent, with hot showers, plenty of toilets and even a swimming pool for the hotter days. It can be cold off-season, so make sure you bring a good sleeping bag if planning to camp in the autumn or winter. It is open February to November but in summer it is best to book. There is also Mar-Oct camping in the village of Samoreau near Montereau (11 Rue Eglise, 77210 Samoreau), and camping at Grez-sur-Loing in the southern area at Camping LES PRÉS (Chemin des Prés, 77880, Grez-sur-Loing).

❐ *La Musardière camping*

❒ Cul de Chien > Yellow Circuit

Everyone should arrange travel and health insurance before coming to Fontainebleau, bouldering can be dangerous and accidents do happen. Make sure you have basic first aid equipment with you and take plenty of skin cream, fingertape, painkillers, antiseptic cream and just generally look after yourself. Bouldering is intensive and even small injuries can ruin a trip. Should you need an ambulance, dial 15. For Police, dial 17. Check your landings and make sure you have learnt the essential art of spotting, it is an expected skill. Take as big a mat as you can manage, or rent one from the outdoor shops in Fontainebleau, or from the cafe at Arbonne.

❐ Look after each other

On rainy or over-hot days when you can't climb, it is an opportunity to rest and visit the artist museums in Barbizon, the chateaux, or simply explore the way-marked 'Denecourt' trails in the forest with their feature rocks. Use the IGN walking maps of the forest (available in newsagents in Milly, Barbizon etc). The walks are all colour-coded such as the excellent red trail *Sentier des 25 Bosses* which tours the Trois Pignons high ground, or the picturesque shorter routes such as the *Sentier Bleu 16*. When it gets too hot, there are swimming pools at Buthiers and Musardière campsite in the summer.

❐ Walk some of the trails

The first and most essential purchase is the IGN map of *Forêt de Fontainebleau* (2417 OT), which is ideal for navigating the trails. Fontainebleau bouldering can be found on the web, with many good sites such as *www.bleau.info* or the official COSIROC club site *www.cosiroc.fr*. Weather is crucial for bouldering here, with cold dry conditions vital for success, so check the 'meteo' on the back page of *Le Parisien* newspaper, or purloin one at the local cafe. The best conditions can be found from October to April, the summer is often too hot to climb.

❐ The cakes of Milly-la-Forêt

Food is the main culture in France and you can eat well from the excellent small village shops, which open in the morning about 8am and shut for a few hours in the afternoon. Many shops and supermarkets are shut on Sundays and Monday afternoons, so beware! Markets are excellent (Milly-la-Forêt on a Sunday and Thursday) and all food and climbing supplies (Decathlon) can be found at the giant Carrefour retail park 5km north of Cuvier off the N7 north of Chailly-en-Bière. There are supermarkets at Milly and Chapelle La Reine. Pharmacies are common (green crosses) and essential for skin-cream!

❐ Paul Roberts on La Voie Michaud > Éléphant

Ethics & Rules of Play

☑ BE RESPECTFUL! The forest of Fontainebleau is a Biosphere Reserve and nature should always come first. Move on if you come across birds nesting, snakes and lizards basking on rocks etc. Try not to go off-piste too often as erosion is becoming a problem on such a sandy soil.

☑ NO LITTER! Please respect the forest and leave no food litter, finger-tape, brushes, excess chalk, plastic, cigarette butts etc. Take any litter you find away.

☑ DO NOT SHOUT and howl when you fail or succeed – many other people come to enjoy the solitude of the forest and satisfaction is best savoured to yourself.

☑ NO DAMAGING ROCK! No chipping of holds – this has been a problem in the past and is absolutely unacceptable. It is important the rock is respected and if a piece of rock simply isn't climbable to you, just move on. Making it easier by chipping or manufacturing holds will leave you feeling very sorry for yourself.

☑ USE CHALK SPARINGLY and NO 'POF' (resin dust). This is not fashionable and coats the rock with a sticky black goo. To dry holds, a good tip is to use a chalky rag to smack holds. Brush holds before and after use and try not to tick-mark everything to death. Five minutes 'patrol' after your session is worth giving back to the forest.

☑ ETIQUETTE PLEASE! Don't take photographs or videos of climbers and certainly not for Facebook/Twitter etc. without asking permission. Don't jump onto problems if people are working them, take your queue on busy circuits, don't blurt out 'beta' unless asked for and don't crowd out a problem for too long if you are with a group. In other words, give people space and respect. It is all about having a bit of fun as long as it doesn't get in the way of others doing so as well.

☑ NO TO HUMAN WASTE. Try and wait till you get home or back to the campsite. If you are caught short deep in the woods, make sure you bury any waste, usually a sandy hole can be dug. There is nothing more unsightly than a pile of crap and/or toilet paper behind any boulder. Other people use the forest and may be exploring.

Bloc Notes & Safety

☑ Whilst the circuits are all classic examples of technique and fairly consistent within their grade, the test piece problems in this guide are chosen to represent a variety of classic bouldering skills . . . often all at once. The guide is a subjective selection chosen to test all your skills, from butch roofs to fingery slabs to highball mantles. You may also find a certain sequence suits you, or that some problems are a little 'morpho' (dependent on your body size). You may even find an entirely new technique to solve the problem. Just have fun and don't view this guide as prescriptive, we are all different!

☑ Take note of your anticipated landings, descents and jump-offs. Tree roots and embedded rocks can be a real issue, so place mats carefully. 'Spotting' is a crucial skill to develop and give confidence to your friends and help minimise injury. Protect head and back on low roof problems; on higher problems, stand back and prepare to push the falling climber in a safe direction away from trees or boulders. Climbing is always your own responsibility, so take care.

☑ Some problems require specific strengths, or, in the case of traverses; good stamina. Other problems require good friction conditions or finger-strength. The sandstone at Fontainebleau can provide some very condition-dependent 'slopers', or fierce 'matchstick' crimps, making it impossible to climb some problems in the heat, so get up early or return in cool conditions (early morning can be the magic time). Other problems require poise and balance; insisting on a combination of technique, footwork, and composure to complete the problem.

☑ Other problems will have 'secrets' where body position and good technique are as crucial as brute strength and will often serve you better. Some problems can only be completed dynamically. This is a speciality of Fontainebleau and great fun, but often very specific and technical, so watch your landings and aim to 'dead-point' the throw or lunge.

☑ For the higher, committing problems good mental composure, confidence and experience may be required before these problems can be attempted. Plenty of mats may give you confidence, but do not rely on them. If you are on a trip, consider the fact that you can always move on to a safer problem nearby, rather than spend your trip on crutches or worse.

☑ Check your descent!

☑ Spotting is key!

☑ Come prepared!

☑ Take care and stay safe!

Circuits

Fontainebleau is the home of 'circuit' climbing. These colour-coded trails follow an 'Alpine Grade' of difficulty according to colour. Generally white and yellow are for beginners, blue for competent, red for hard, and black (sometimes white) for elite, though many circuits are marked in colours which are distinctive to themselves (e.g. salmon pink, sky blue etc.) A circuit is marked on the rock with discreet numbers and arrows. Usually, a circuit begins at an introductory problem with a painted square or triangle, with a notation of the difficulty. A problem will be marked with an arrow indicating rough direction, maybe bent to the left or right to indicate which way to trend. A traverse is marked by an L-shape arrow, often with spot dabs for where feet go and dashed 'continue' arrows for hands. A final problem is often marked with a solid colour square at the base of the arrow. Try to remember that the circuit problems are made to be linked and descents often lead along intermediary rocks to continuations involving as much rock as possible. There is a deeper logic to the circuits and a great deal of thought has been put into their design to highlight the full range of climbing styles and techniques.

◇ F: *facile* (easy) > Easier angles and larger holds, interlinked with easy rock. Yellow circuits or white kids' circuits, mainly Font 1/2.

◆ PD: *peu difficile* (not very difficult) > a little more complex, technical and with higher, longer circuits up to Font 3. Alpine 'yellow' circuits and some long orange trails.

◆ AD: *assez difficile* (fairly difficult) > expect some hardish problems, technical slabs, walls, cracks and maybe exposed in places. Orange circuits up to Font 3+/4.

◆ D: *difficile* (difficult) > more serious walls, slabs, and steeper ground. Highly technical and fingery. Stamina becomes a real issue. Mainly blue circuits and some red circuits: Font 4 , 4+ and 5.

◆ TD: *très difficile* (very difficult) > hard, varied red circuits mostly: technical, 'stopper' walls, traverses, roofs, arêtes etc. Font 4+ to 6b.

◆ ED1/2/3/4: *extrêmement difficile* (extremely difficult) > varied, elite black or white circuits, rarely completed except by 'Bleausards' (local experts): Font 6a to 8a.

☑ Circuit start

☑ Follow the numbers

☑ R-L traverse and then up

☑ Repainted circuit

❐ *Yellow circuit at 91.1*

❐ Chris Houston on the classic 'Rubis sur l' Ongles > Gorge Aux Chats > 7b+

Grades

The modern 'Fontainebleau' grade is based on the French numerical grading system, though it has developed very much its own 'flavour'. It has grades from 1 to 9 and each number is divided into 'a, b, c' increments of difficulty e.g. Font 7a, Font 7b, Font 7c. These have further additive + *supérieur* grades such as 7a+, which is the grade between 7a and 7b.

It is not usefully comparative to the popular French sports grading (a 'Font 7a' is very different to a sport-grade 'French 7a'). On first visit, the grades will be a shock to your system as you slip off Font 3s and 4s, (even the 8a climber will do this). The rock is technical and does not give up its grades easily. The grading chart here reflects a rough comparison of various international grading systems, should you wish to translate your 'home' grade. Traverses are graded for overall difficulty rather than a single move.

Circuits are graded with an Alpine grade, such as AD+, to give an overall sense of severity, though grades will vary within the circuit problems. It is best to view the grading system as a sliding scale of difficulty as grades can be very subjective, due to the erosion or breakage of holds, polish, body-size and, especially at Fontainebleau: conditions!

The Stone Country Bouldering Conversion Chart

(A rough guide to bouldering levels)

FONT	VERMIN	BRITISH	ALPINE
		3a	F
2	V0	3b	
		3c	
3			PD
		4a	
3+	V0+		
		4b	AD
4			
		4c	D
4+			
	VI	5a	
5			
		5b	
5+	V2		
		5c	TD
6a			
	V3	6a	
6b			
	V4		ED
6c		6b	
	V5		
7a			
	V6	6c	
7a+	V7		
7b			
7b+	V8	7a	
7c	V9		
7c+	V10		
8a	V11		
8a+	V12		
8b	V13	7b	
8b+	V14		
8c	V15		
8c+/9a	V16	7c	

Notation Notes

Contractions used in this guide include: **SS** (a Sitting Start); **CS** (a Crouching Start); **RH** (Right Hand); **LH** (Left Hand). The topo lines have a solid start circle if a sit start and a transparent circle if standing. Topo circuits starts are marked with a ◇ diamond and feature problems (listed in ascending grades) are marked with **A** green alphabetic letters on the topo.

History

The forest of Fontainebleau is the alchemy of everything the boulderer holds dear: physicality, technique, attractive stone, variety, solitude and landscape. Anyone who is inspired by movement in climbing should come here at least once and sample the subtle treasures that are found in the forest.

Thousands upon thousands of boulders lie scattered on the sandy rolling hills ('pignons'), amidst 280 km^2 of pine, beech, chestnut, birch and oak woods. Development of the hardest technical moves on the planet continues, with the current grade of 8c being the heady elixir for the most talented *Bleausards*. Most of the forest's boulders have now had over a century of development and exploration, despite this a strong French ethic of conservation and egalitarianism has meant the forest still enchants the visitor with a sense of openness. The circuits are marked discreetly and even the popular areas retain their magic and reclusive formulae for success.

The forest is really a manmade environment imposed on an older geological enigma. It is thought the boulders tumbled from plateaux of petrified sand-dunes, formed in the Oligocene era 20-30 million years ago. These have since been eroded into fantastical, 'sculpted' landmarks such as *Le Diplodocus, L'Éléphant, Le Bilboquet, L'Aerolithe, The Kissing Serpents* etc.

Petroglyphs found on the rocks suggest it was a rich hunting ground for humans in the stone ages. Since the 13th century, when a hunting dog named 'Blaud' supposedly discovered a 'fountain' in the largely arid forest, a succession of kings and emperors had used the forest as a royal hunting ground until the 1789 Revolution returned the forest to the civil status it enjoys today.

Mapping the forest began in the 1830s when Claude-François Denecourt linked his colour-coded walks through the rocky features of the forest. Many distinctive boulders were pit-stops on these trails and it was no surprise that people began to climb these 'alphabet rocks'. The mountaineering clubs were perhaps the first to develop this idea further. 1908 was a significant year when Alpine Club members began to string together routes on the boulders to practice technique for the higher mountains. The yellow and orange circuits in the forest often imitate these early trails, where there is a lot of scrambling on rock between ascents of easy, but often high, pillars and distinctive featured rocks. This 'circuit climbing' would gradually become more evolved.

❒ The 'grès' sandstone of Fontainebleau

❒ Get to know your paths . . .

❒ The forest in Denecourt's time

So began an inexorable trend and the boulders began to attract more focus as technical abilities increased. In 1934 Pierre Allain climbed *La Fissure des Alpinistes* (the first Font 5) at Apremont and a year later added *L'Angle Allain* (5+) at Cuvier Rempart. He also introduced rubber-soled climbing boots to improve adhesion. The first recorded circuit was the red circuit at Cuvier Rempart in 1947, which echoed Denecourt's walking circuits – painting numbers and arrows on the problems to create a 'training' circuit of varying problems. These circuits were supposed to hone technique for the higher mountains but eventually became popular in their own right. The individual problems in the forest began to grow more technical and divorced from their circuit origins, requiring sometimes months of effort and refined strength.

'Bas Cuvier' is perhaps the heart of this Fontainebleau dedication. The whole area has a distinguished bouldering history. In 1908 Jacques Wehrlin climbed, in nailed boots, *La Fissure Wehrlin* – a Font 3 chimney left of *Duroxmanie*. 1914 saw Jacques de Lepiney climb the high crack of *La Prestat*. In 1935, Cuvier Rempart saw Pierre Allain (soled with his own rubber 'PAs') climb the slippery *Angle Allain* (5+), and in 1946 René Ferlet climbed *La Marie Rose* – the first 6a in the forest and a masterclass in the bouldering art. In 1953 Robert Paragot succeeded on *La Joker* (given 6c at the time) and in 1960 Michel Libert climbed *Abattoir*, which has now crept close to 7a+ as a consensus grade. In 1977, Jérome Jean-Charles climbed the first forest 7b of *Carnage*, a modern power problem. Next to it, *L'Abbé Résina* was the first 7c, climbed in 1983 by Pierre Richard. In 1984 Jacky Godoffe opened the eighth grade with *C'Était Demain*, and Cuvier and its backwoods 'remparts' sees no sign of relinquishing its cutting-edge status.

Current development continues on remote and hidden blocs within the forest, such as Dave Graham's 8b+ *The Island* at Coquibus, extended by Vincent Pochon to give *The Big Island* 8c. *Jour de Chasse* is a 2013 8c from Jan Hojer at the Recloses venue. As for traversing, the grades have here crept up to 9a (not like a 'bloc 9a'), the highlight of which recently has been Jean-Pierre Bouvier's 2012 ascent of *Fou Rire aller/retour* which was climbed when he was 55 years of age.

Fontainebleau may now have a heavy footfall in terms of boulderers, but solitude and spirit can still be found in the forest. Take with you a sense of history and respect for the rocks and the people who have nurtured the bouldering in Fontainebleau – it is a precious environment and if we look after it will provide bouldering for all our future generations.

❐ *L'Angle Allain*

❐ *La Bérézina (L'Abbé Résina) at Cuvier*

❐ *The forest is watching you . . .*

❒ *La Marie Rose* > the first 6a at Cuvier > Photo © John Sharples

TROIS PIGNONS

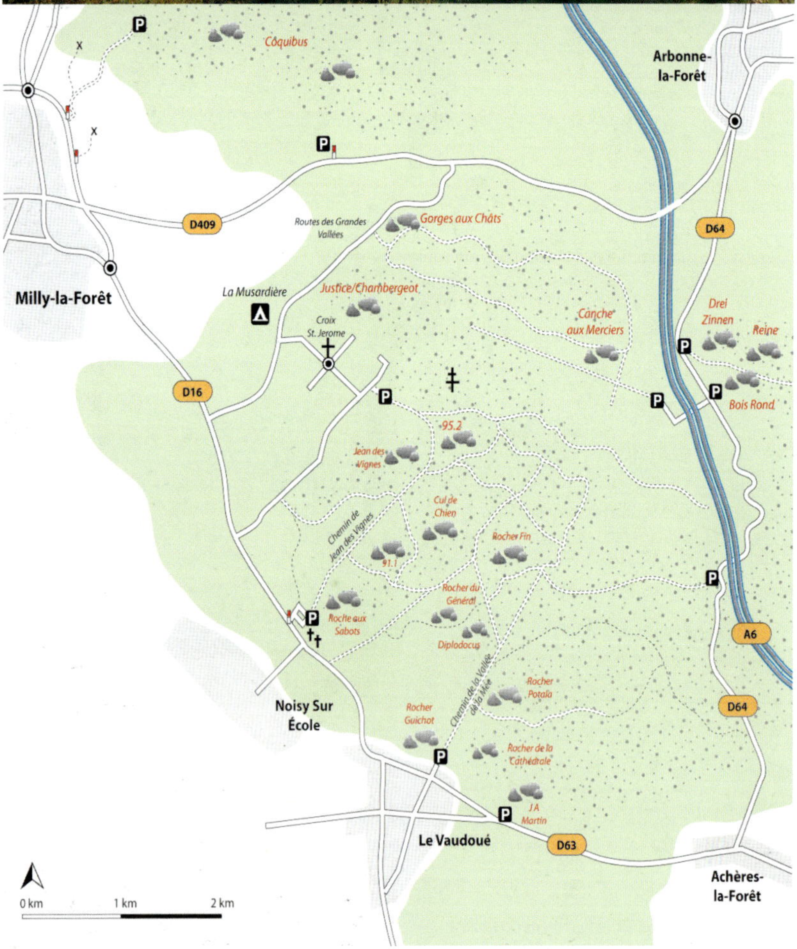

TROIS PIGNONS

These superb bouldering venues known collectively as the Trois Pignons lie on a vast sandy desert with pine and birch trees surrounding beautifully clean sandstone boulders. It is probably the best area to visit first, as it has an open and friendly atmosphere. It is both a place to visit alone or with friends – walking in from Croix St. Jerome, perhaps after a long drive, the spirit is lifted immediately with the glimpse of sun-dappled boulders on the sandy hills. It is a magical place that forges a strong urge for future return.

❒ Le Bilboquet

Trois Pignons translates roughly as 'three peaks' and it captures the spirit of stone and forest together. The whole circular forest plain is skirted by the excellent full-day walk of the red-waymarked *Sentier des 25 Bosses,* which completes all the highest points in the massif including the three peaks east of the Croix St. Jerome car parks. It is a fantastic walk in itself and a great way to familiarise yourself with the network of 'chemins' and the complex bouldering areas. Bear in mind that erosion can be a problem and do not add to it by taking unnecessary shortcuts or ignoring the conservation areas – they are there for a reason.

The area is famous for the picturesque 'Mer de Sable' sands of the Cul de Chien area, where the classic roof problem *Le Toît du Cul de Chien* still provides a meaty and highball test of your mettle. For the main, western areas in the Trois Pignons, most people base themselves at La Musardière campsite, from where it is a fifteen minute walk to the Croix St. Jerome car-parks and the entrance to the forest. From here you reach the first area of *95.2* (the height of the hill gives this place its name) in about ten minutes along the *Chemin de la Vallée Close.* From here, the other areas are no more than 10 or 15 minutes walk. If you get lost, follow the tracks west back to the main artery of the *Chemin de la Plaine de Jean des Vignes* which links the Croix St. Jérome car-park with the Roche aux Sabots car park.

❒ Yellow circuit at 95·2

❒ Retour aux Sources at 95·2

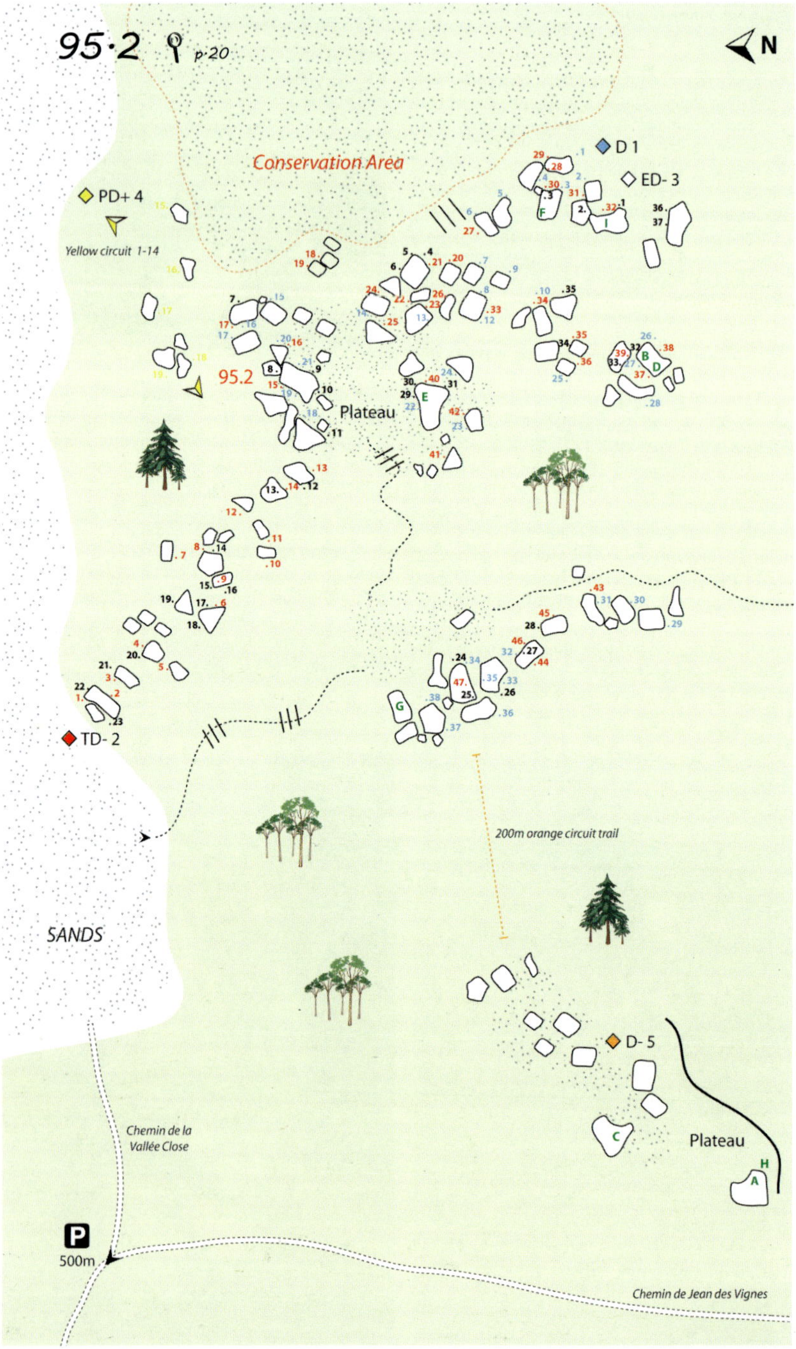
95·2
p·20
N
Conservation Area
◇ PD+ 4
Yellow circuit 1-14
◆ D 1
◇ ED- 3
95.2
Plateau
◆ TD- 2
200m orange circuit trail
SANDS
◆ D- 5
Plateau
Chemin de la Vallée Close
P
500m
Chemin de Jean des Vignes

95·2

BLOC NOTES >>> 95.2 is the height of the hill upon which these fast-drying boulders stand. This is probably the first area you will visit if staying at the Musardière campsite, as it is only twenty minutes walk through the luxurious forest houses of Croix St. Jerome. The hill has a number of excellent circuits and some classic test pieces, some of the 7a problems are still world-class despite their age. The beautiful central outlook from the summit over the Trois Pignons makes this a popular spot and it can be busy at weekends. Please adhere to the fenced-off conservation zones, as the sandy hill is very prone to erosion.

ACCESS >>> For the *Croix St. Jerome* forest car-park, turn off the *Grandes Vallées* road 200m south of the campsite and continue for 1km over the roundabout (with a cross in the centre) to a forest track to the parking. An 800m walk east along the *Chemin de la Vallée Close* leads to open sands under a long, ridged hill with the double-cross monument on the left. Head up the hill on the right (from the sands) via a heathery path to the top of the hill, which leads you to the central *Ectoplasme* area of 95.2 from where a low ridge extends west. The summit of the hill is further uphill on the east at a sandy viewpoint.

CIRCUITS >>> The ◆ yellow circuit (PD+ no. 4) is a fun circuit of 54 problems, starting just off the sandy plain on the NE flank. The ◆ orange circuit (D- no. 5) is a wandering circuit of 40 problems, starting on the far west of the ridge. The ◆ blue circuit (D no. 1) is a classic circuit of 38 clean problems starting on the southern flank of the hill. Nos. 19 (a slab) and 34 (the wall *Ectoplasme*) are representative of the quality of the circuit. The ◆ red circuit TD- no. 2 is another classic of 47 problems starting just off the sandy plain on the north of the hill – nos. 15, 45 and 47 are typical of the technique required. The ◇ white circuit (ED- no. 3) – black numbers on the topo – is a superb circuit of 37 puzzlers starting on the south flank, with 12 variant problems.

TEST PIECES >>>

❒ A. *Duel dans la Lune*	6c	SS cave to slopey ledges & pocket to top. *Rude Boy* goes right at 7a.
❒ B. *Mur de la Fosse aux Ours*	7a	Fine technical wall left of red 37, strong fingers on the 'sugarcube'!
❒ C. *Retour aux Sources*	7a	SS the attractive overhanging blunt prow from an orange cave.
❒ D. *Danses avec les Loups*	7a+	Smear up the slabby arête right of red 37.
❒ E. *Miss KGB*	7a+	The central slopey wall left of big pockets, crimpy to start and polished.
❒ F. *Le Bloc à Bertrand*	7a+	Cracked sandpit wall up to slopers, back right. Direct is *Jête Michaud.*
❒ G. *Pierre Precieuse*	7a+	Hanging groove, dynamically or static (*Le Yaniro*). No arête.
❒ H. *Sans Dessus Dessous*	7b+	*Duel...* but travel left to use arête and slopers to gain top.
❒ I. *Ange Naïf*	7c	The holes right of white 1. Direct 7c jump, or crimp right at 7a+.

❒ The Orange Circuit

❒ Blue 18

❐ 95·2 landscape

❐ 95·2 > White 25

❐ 95·2 > Jête Michaud

❐ 95·2 > White 37

❐ 95·2 > Duel Bloc

❐ 95·2 > 'La Fosse aux Ours'

❐ 95·2 > Miss KGB bloc

❐ 95·2 > Ectoplasme bloc

❐ Gorge aux Chats > S' Appelle aux Logis

❐ Gorge aux Chats > Grêve des Nains

❐ Gorge aux Chats > Red 17

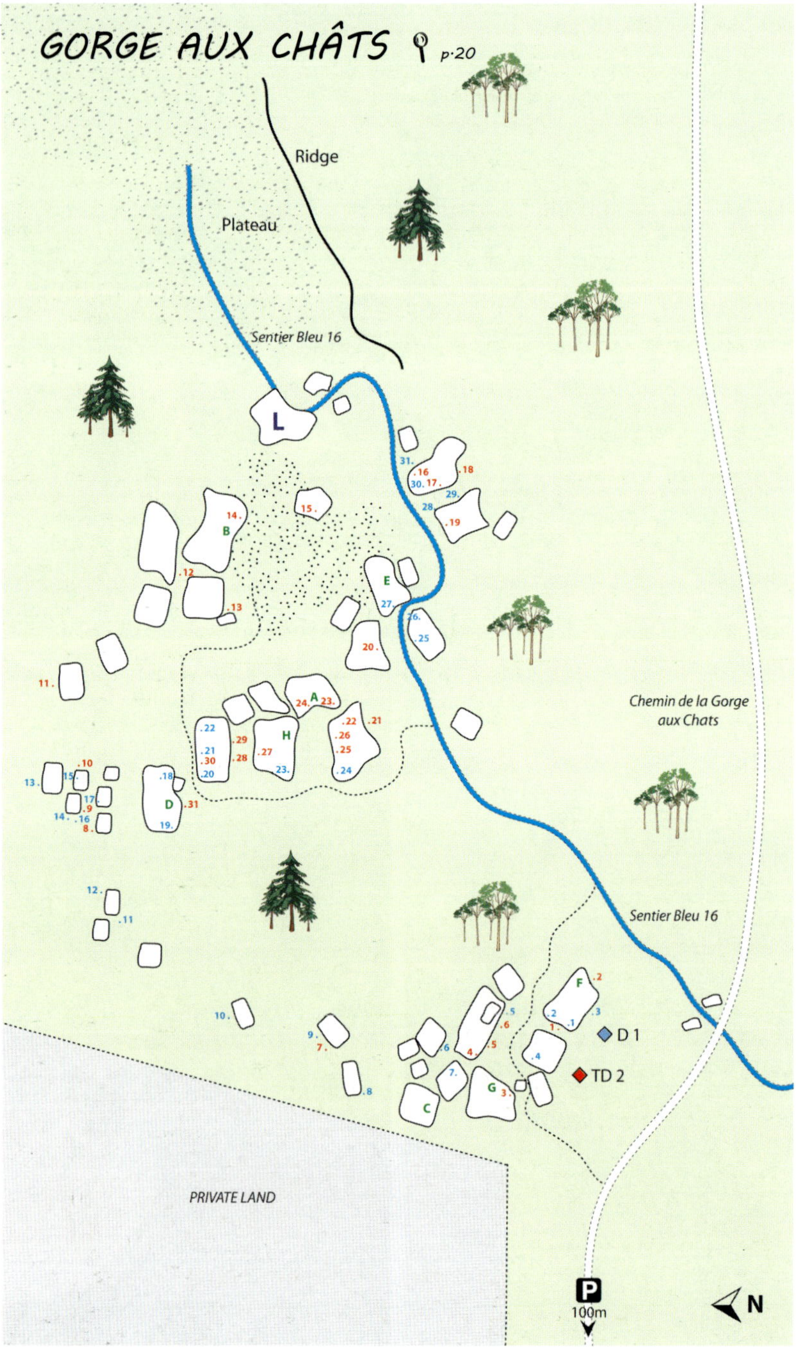
GORGE AUX CHÂTS
p.20
Ridge
Plateau
Sentier Bleu 16
L
B
E
A
H
D
F
G
C
Chemin de la Gorge aux Chats
Sentier Bleu 16
D 1
TD 2
PRIVATE LAND
P
100m
N

GORGE AUX CHÂTS

BLOC NOTES >>> 'The gorge of the chestnuts' (not cats) has a secluded and pleasant feel, and is close to the Musardière campsite. Situated on a high bluff above the Milly plain, it has a fine outlook from the summit rocks. The name of the area refers to the 'chataignes' or spiky chestnuts you will see everywhere in autumn. Of more relevance to the climber is the select number of classic problems, including the famous grooved wall of *Rubis sur l'Ongle* which caught the world's attention briefly when it was climbed in 1991 and is one of the most sought-after problems in the forest. The *Sentier Bleu 16* is a good reference-marker trail and it winds uphill from the valley path through the boulders here and is a pleasant walk in itself to Canche aux Merciers and back. As this area is above private housing, please respect privacy – park out of sight by the white gate and try not to be noisy.

ACCESS >>> From the D409 Fontainebleau-Milly road, about 2 kilometres east of Milly and just east of the Coquibus auberge, take the Grandes Vallées B-road south – this has a large signpost for Noisy and the *Musardière* campsite amongst other attractions. This junction lies on a bend, so slow down and watch out for oncoming traffic. After 1km and a couple of bends, an open sandy layby area beside a fenced-off house is where you park just past a white gate on the left. Follow the *Chemin de la Gorge aux Chats* into the forest for 200m until the first boulders appear on the left beside a fence. The main area is higher up the hill, follow the blue markers of the SB16 from the main path. The main area is quick drying as it lies on a ridge.

CIRCUITS >>> The ◆ blue circuit (D no. 1) is a round of 31 problems, nowhere too difficult, but varied. Best are 24 & 27. The ◆ red circuit (TD no. 2) is a classic little circuit of 31 tough problems, with some good variant problems such as the classic *Travaux Forcés*. Also good are red 14, 17, 18,19, 23, 28 and the classic 6a of Red 31 known as *Grêve des Nains*.

TEST PIECES >>>

❒ A. *Travaux Forcés*	6b	Red 23 bis, traverse into the ochre groove to a hard twist to the high jug.
❒ B. *Arachnée*	6b	Traverse the juggy roof from right to left, follow the arrows all the way.
❒ C. *Les Mains Pleines*	6c+	SS square roof via crack, gain slopey ledges and mantle out left. R is 7a+.
❒ D. *Grêve des Nains*	7a	SS the cave ramp (no jugs over lip) to gain the shield wall of red 31.
❒ E. *S'Appelle au Logis*	7a	SS in cave, gain arête, move left to pockets over plinth to slopey top.
❒ F. *Neige d'Automne*	7a	SS red 2 and finish up slopey right arête. Cave SS to right is *Magneton* 7c+.
❒ G. *Le Pare Dessus*	7a+	Low roof right of red 3. Travel left to mantle onto slab, or finish up arête.
❒ H. *Rubis Sur l'Ongles*	7b+	Absolute classic groove, very polished finger holds at start.

❒ *Backwoods traversing*

❒ *Travaux Forcés*

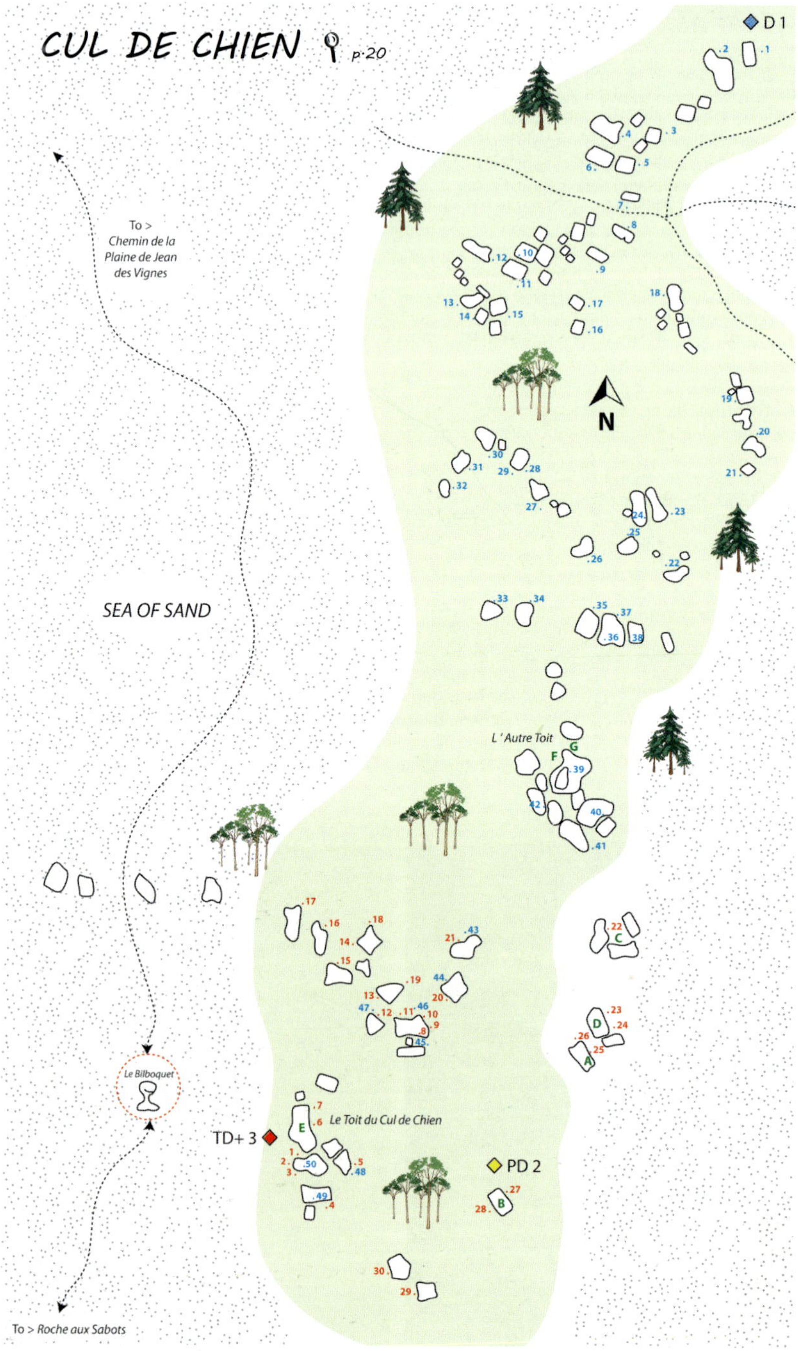
CUL DE CHIEN
p.20
D 1
To >
Chemin de la
Plaine de Jean
des Vignes
N
SEA OF SAND
L'Autre Toit
Le Bilboquet
Le Toit du Cul de Chien
TD+ 3
PD 2
To > Roche aux Sabots

CUL DE CHIEN

BLOC NOTES >>> The famous *Cul de Chien* area is popular as the large sandy sea in the middle of the forest has some excellent open boulders with good circuit problems. The hard-core climber should head straight for the 'Autre Toit' (the 'other roof') which has a selection of testpieces into the eighth grade. From the parking, it is a 20 minute walk to the pleasant open sands of Cul de Chien, where the famous *Tête de Chien/Le Bilboquet (*shaped like a dog's head*)* stands in the middle of a large sandy bay. Just to the east of this is a large boulder behind which is the classic roof problem *Toit du Cul de Chien*. This is a good reference point. Most of the circuit problems lie on lower boulders to the north and east of the sands.

ACCESS >>>

1. From the *Croix St. Jérome* car-park: walk along the *Chemin de la Vallée Close* for a few hundred meters then veer right onto the *Chemin de la Plaine de Jean des Vignes*. Pass an open area junction with boulders on the right and continue to a crossroads with the *Chemin de Mont Pivot*. From here, turn east (left) into the forest along a path which leads to the sands, turn right and head vaguely uphill to a sandy pass, where you will see the *Tête de Chien* (aka *Le Bilboquet* boulder). The main area is to the east (left).

2. From the *Roche aux Sabots* car park: follow the main *Jean des Vignes* path for 400m to a crossroads. Turn right onto the sandy *Chemin de Roche aux Sabots*. Continue uphill to a junction at the top, turn left onto the sea of sands. Continue across this to *Le Bilboquet* and turn right to the main boulders.

CIRCUITS >>> The repainted ◇ yellow circuit (PD no. 2) has 58 problems, starting just off the sandy plain on the NE flanks, leading north in a long loop. The ◆ blue circuit (D no. 1) is a superb circuit of 53 problems starting at the far north of the area, ends at *Le Toit* area. The ◆ red circuit (TD+ no. 3) has 30 problems (and 3 variants) starting just east of the *Bilboquet*. Highlights: 1, 3, 6, 7, 10, 14, 15, 18, 19, 21, 22, 27, 30.

TEST PIECES >>>

❒ A. *Doléance*	6a	Red 25 bis. A tricky Cul de Chien slab left of red 25.
❒ B. *Verglas Frequent*	6b	Red 27. Desperate little slab problem, crimpy, sticky toes.
❒ C. *Hammer's Break*	6c	Red 22 bis. Undercut problem finishing direct, no stacking mats.
❒ D. *Belle Lurette*	7a	Slab left of red 23.
❒ E. *Le Toit du Cul de Chien*	7a	The famous roof through the drilled pockets to a highball groove.
❒ F. *Arabesque*	7b+	Undercut the roof (kneebar) to the pocket to slopey finish left.
❒ G. *Éclipse*	7c	Undercut roof niche left round to the hanging crack. Subtle power.

❒ *Arabesque*

❒ *Le Toit du Cul de Chien*

❒ *Yellow circuit*

❒ Cul de Chien > Le Toit

❒ Cul de Chien > Blue 29

❒ Cul de Chien > Blue 45

❒ Cul de Chien > Yellow circuit

❒ Cul de Chien > L' Autre Toit

❐ 91·1 > Cure Dents

❐ 91·1 > Chain descent

❐ 91·1 > Ingratitude (red 9)

❐ 91·1 > Le Surplomb Ocre

❐ 91·1 > Le Flippeur

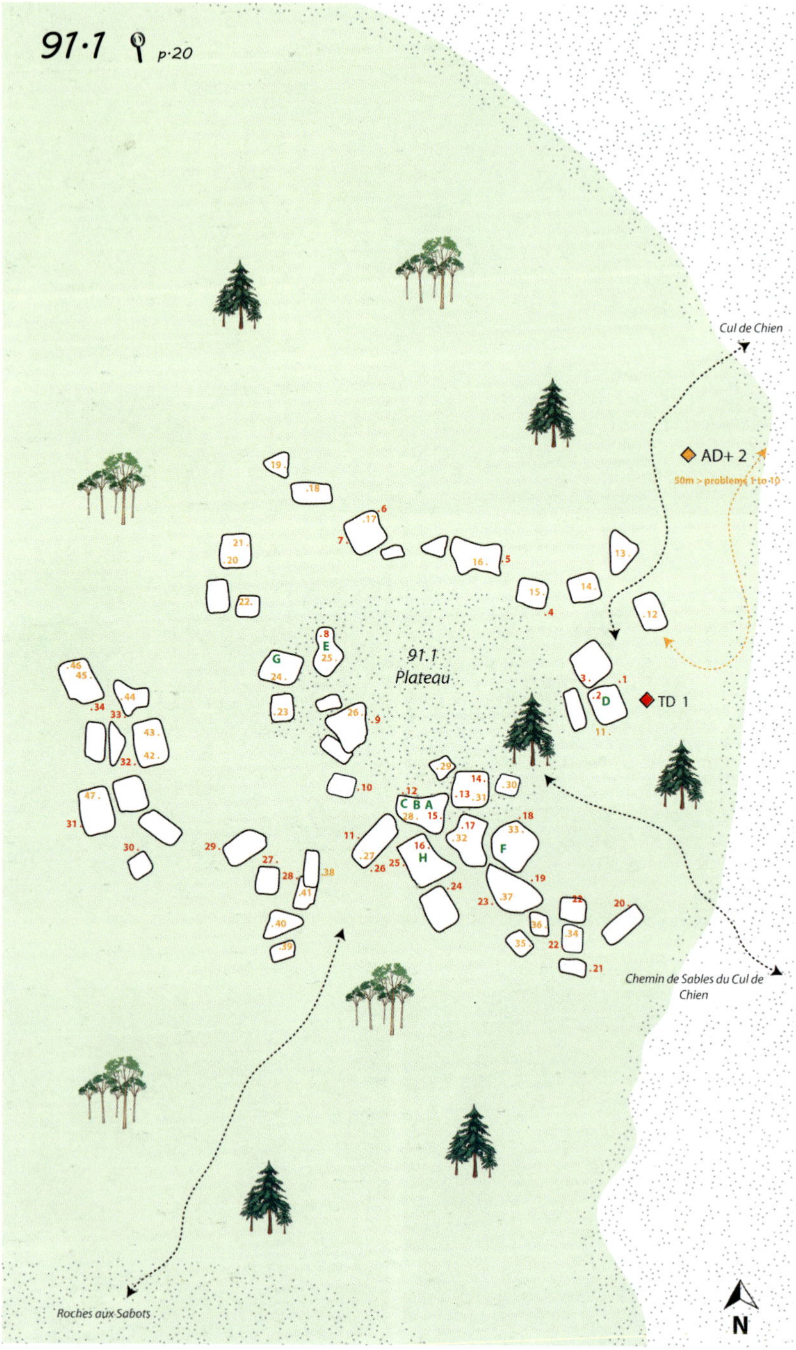

91·1
p·20
Cul de Chien
AD+ 2
50m > problems 1 to 10
TD 1
91.1
Plateau
Chemin de Sables du Cul de Chien
Roches aux Sabots
N

91·1

BLOC NOTES >>> *91.1* is another fine hill with boulders, located just opposite Cul du Chien - across the sands westwards. It has a number of fine slabs and walls, but few test pieces. The red circuit is well worth a visit. The area is elevated and sandy and dries quickly. For the giant ochre roof, it is worth taking a top-rope if you decide to do it!

ACCESS >>> If you're at Cul de Chien, cross the sands westwards past *Le Bilboquet* to the top of the wooded hill. If you are parked at the Roche aux Sabots car-park, walk 500m along the *Chemin de la Plaine de Jean des Vignes* and turn right up the sandy track of the *Chemin Roche aux Sabots*. As this reaches a sandy clearing and a fork at the top of the hill, turn left across yellow sand and flat blocks into the woods and head uphill to the main boulders.

CIRCUITS >>> There are two orange circuits here – the ◆ (AD+ no. 2) circuit starts on the downhill, eastern side of the main area and has 47 problems and 5 variants. The ◆ (AD no. 4) circuit starts on the west side at the first clearing on approach from the *Chemin de la Plaine de Jean des Vignes*. The ◆ red (TD no.1) circuit has 34 super technical problems, many of them slabs and walls, including the must-do *L'Arc de Cercle* (12 bis).

❒ *Red 2 bis*

TEST PIECES >>>

❒ A. *Arc de Cercle*	5+	Red 12 bis. The curving crack, descend by chain.
❒ B. *Le Grand Dièdre*	6a	Red 12 ter. The grooved corner right of crack.
❒ C. *Le Cure-Dents*	6a	Red 12. The excellent right arête.
❒ D. *La Pince*	6b	Red 2 bis. Left side of arête, pinch and go to top pocket.
❒ E. *Le Flippeur Assis*	7a	Sit start of the pillar of red 8 bis. 6b stand.
❒ F. *Le Surplomb Ocre*	7a	Sit start to right of red 18 and climb orange roof via pockets.
❒ G. *Le Sous-plomb*	7a+	Sit start low roof to right of red 8.
❒ H. *L'Américain*	7b	Sit start roof and mantle right of red 16.

❒ *Red 2*

❒ *Red 9*

❒ *91·1 rock*

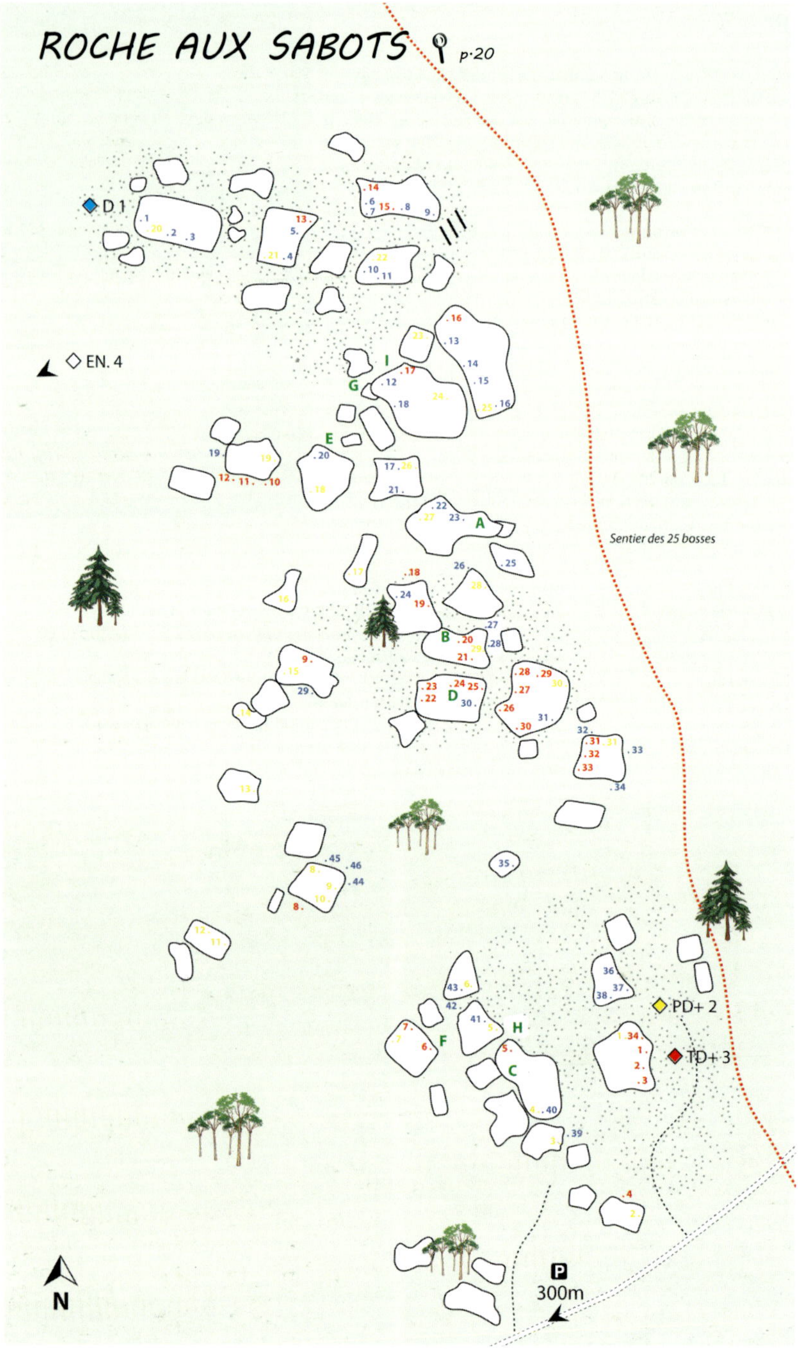
ROCHE AUX SABOTS
p.20
D1
EN. 4
Sentier des 25 bosses
PD+ 2
TD+ 3
P
300m
N

ROCHE AUX SABOTS

BLOC NOTES >>> 'Sabots' is one of the most accessible and popular of the forest's venues, and deservedly so. The rock is clean and the problems are almost every one of them a classic. It can get very busy, especially on school outings, so try to visit at a quiet time in the morning or evening, you'll benefit from cooler conditions on the polished crimps and slopers. The landings are mostly very sandy, but watch out for tree roots and make sure your spotting skills are attentive. At weekends, climbing supplies are available from the small van usually parked at the start of the *Jean des Vignes* path.

ACCESS >>> From the large car-park just before the cemetery if driving from Milly to Le Vaudoué. Park in the NE corner – from here the popular *Chemin de la Plaine de Jean des Vignes* leads off northwards. There are two approaches: 1. Blue Circuit start: take *Jean de Vignes* path for 200m then veer right at white kids' circuit boulders to the larger boulders further into the wooded hill. 2. Red Circuit start: the east side of the boulderfield. Take take the small track that goes right off the start of *Jean des Vignes*, this path veers left and reaches the boulders in 200 metres on the left.

CIRCUITS >>> A ◇ white kids' circuit (EN no. 4) starts from *Jean des Vignes* side of the boulderfield. The ◇ yellow circuit (PD+ no. 2) is a sometimes highball circuit of 31 problems and 6 bis, starting in the south-east of the boulderfield: highlights are 6, 7, 8, 13. The classic ◆ blue circuit (D no. 1) has 46 varied and delightful problems (and 5 var.), highlights being 3, 10, 12, 16, 24, 29, 36, 40 – start at the north-west end off *Jean des Vignes*. The ◆ red circuit (TD+ no. 3) is a technical classic with 34 problems and 14 desperate variants, starting in the south-east plain. Highlights on this superb, technical circuit are: 3, 6, 7, 13, 14, 20, 22, 23, 25, 28, 29, 34, most problems are in the 5 to 6b range. There are many historic 7th grade variants.

TEST PIECES >>>

❒ A. *Le Chapeau Chinois*	6b	Red 18 bis roof. The 'chinese hat' breaking out left through slopers.
❒ B. *Bazooka Jo*	6c	Red 20 bis. In corridor, red & white arrow. A fingery, bridging exercise.
❒ C. *Graviton*	7a	Wall in corridor. Layback up good holds then grovel over the top direct.
❒ D. *À l'Impossible…*	7a+	Red 24 bis. Crimpy slab between red 24 and 25, exit right.
❒ E. *Jeu de Toit*	7a+	Pocketed overhang direct to slopey arête, left var. is 6c+ *Anglomaniaque*.
❒ F. *Smash*	7b	Big dyno from ledge to top, left of red 6.
❒ G. *Niveau Baisse*	7b+	SS the overhanging arête right of Blue 12. Stand is *Le Flippeur* 7a.
❒ H. *Sale Gosse*	7c	Hanging roof left of red 5 via slopey pockets and dynamic throws. SS 8a.
❒ I. *Déviation*	8a	The wall left of blue 12.

❒ *Yellow circuit*

❒ *Blue 10*

❒ *Blue 23*

❒ *Red 2*

❒ Sabots > Bazooka Jo > Red 20 bis

❒ Sabots > Graviton

❒ Sabots > Red circuit

❒ Sabots > Le Tiroir > Red 22

❒ Sabots > Red 6

❐ Sabots > Red circuit

❐ Sabots > Le Flippeur/Niveau Baisse (ss)

❐ Sabots > Yellow 6

❐ Sabots > Sale Gosse

❐ Sabots > Amanite Dalloide > Red 19

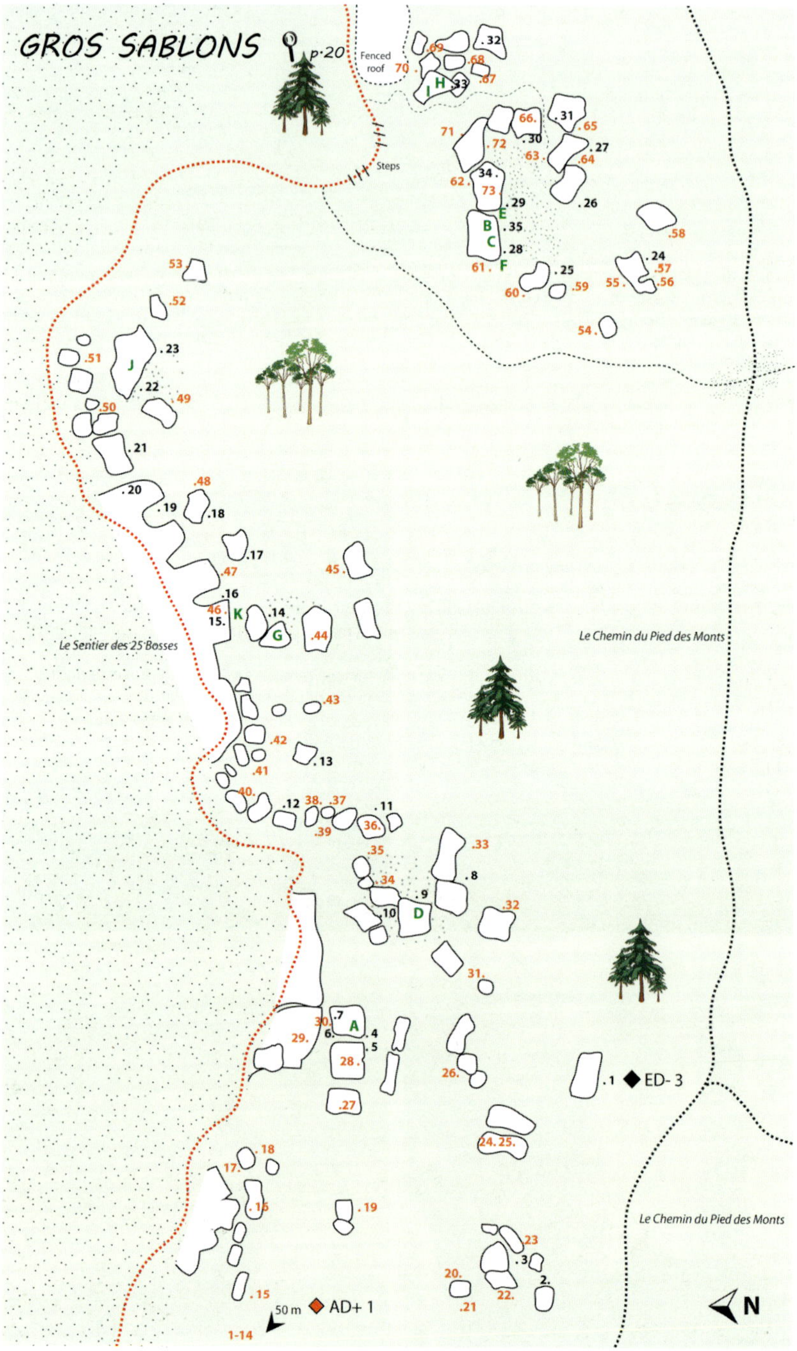
GROS SABLONS
p.20
Fenced roof
Steps
Le Sentier des 25 Bosses
Le Chemin du Pied des Monts
Le Chemin du Pied des Monts
ED- 3
50 m
AD+ 1
1-14
N

GROS SABLONS

BLOC NOTES >>> This central Trois Pignons venue has some highball problems and awkward landings. That said, there are some fine classic problems on the excellent black circuit and the older circuits (blue and orange are good as well). The boulders and walls lie just under the winding ridge path of the red-marked *Sentier des 25 Bosses*. The rock is heavily marbled and excellently technical.

ACCESS >>> From the Croix St. Jerome car-park, follow the *Chemin de la Vallée Close* all the way to the big sandy area. Cross this, skirting the *95.2* hill edge on the right of the sands, past the *Chemin du Cassis* junction to a crossroads, with the 95.2 yellow circuit rocks on your right. Go straight on to the *Chemin du Pied des Monts* path which leads in 500m to a sign (118) on the left at a junction. The black circuit starts on a bloc behind the sign and the boulders and walls lie under the ridge above. For *La Liberté* sector continue on for another 200m to a sandy junction and follow a path uphill left to join the red *Sentier des 25 Bosses* path. Go up the steps on the right and at a fenced-off roof turn off right and skirt the boulders down to a hidden clearing surrounded by beautiful marbled walls . . . the famous crack (6b) is marked very obviously.

CIRCUITS >>> A ◆ 'Bleausard' circuit (ED- no. 3) is a classic trail of 39 problems, often highball, from 4+ to 6c+, it starts just north of the *Pied des Monts/Melun* junction on a slabby wall, then heads up to boulders under the ridge via a large shot-holed boulder, it then continues east under the ridge to cross a valley to the famous *Liberté* area. There is also a long west to east ◆ orange circuit (AD+ no. 1) of 73 problems (and 26 variations), starting on the far west of the boulders under the ridge, and an ◆ old blue circuit (D+ no. 4) of 32 problems plus 12 var. starting beside the black circuit start.

TEST PIECES >>>

❐ A. *La Piscine*	6a	Black 4 highball arête, on boulder right of the twin with big hole.
❐ B. *La Pipicaca*	6b	Black 35 wall to right of *La Liberté*.
❐ C. *La Liberté*	6c	The striking high crack of black 35 bis, it has its name painted on the wall.
❐ D. *L'Oeil de Cyclone*	7a	Through arch to wall on left marked with a black arrow, finish up black 9.
❐ E. *La Grande Arête*	7a	To the right of black 35.
❐ F. *La Rampe*	7a	To the left of black 28, the slopey ramp. Jump start and traverse right.
❐ G. *Casus Belli*	7a+	To the left of black 14, just right of overhanging arête.
❐ H. *Loup Garou*	7b	50m above black 35. Marbled wall just left of corner of black 33.
❐ I. *Hurlement*	7c+	Traverse lip left of *Loup Garou*, finish up arête.
❐ J. *Bibop*	7c+	Bulging marbled wall left of black 23.

❐ La Liberté

❐ The Black Circuit

❐ Hurlement

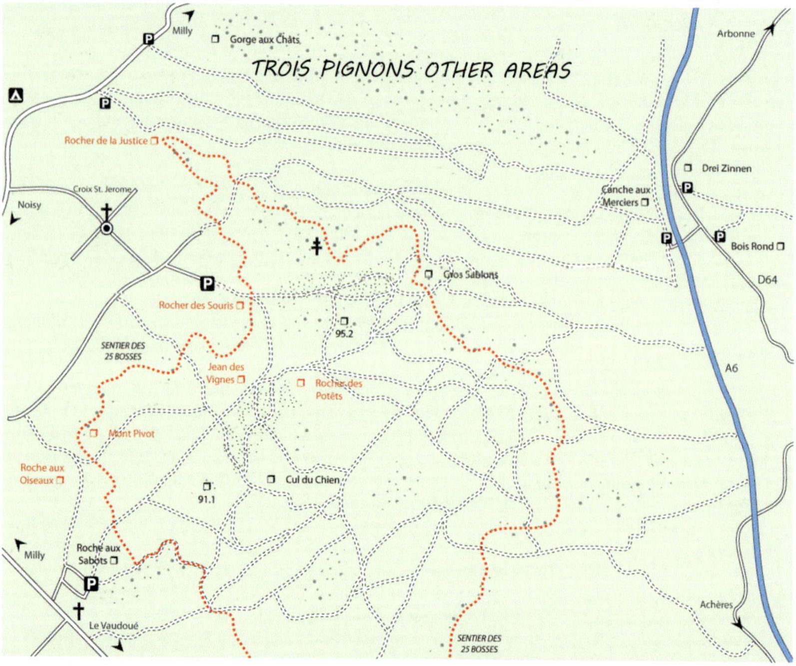

❒ Belle Gueule & Pancras

❒ Oiseaux - Le Mandarin

❒ Souris-Extraction Terrestre

❒ Rocher des Souris - Yogi 7b

❒ Rocher de la Justice - EOS 7b

OTHER AREAS

This area roughly includes the distinctive triplet of hills with dispersed boulders on its eastern flanks above the *Jean des Vignes* path. Some are well worth seeking out for test pieces. It has some isolated boulders and small clusters of boulders outside of the main areas, you are guaranteed a little more solitude here.

Rocher des Souris

The approach is easy, from the car-park at Croix Saint-Jérôme, walk along the *Vallée de la Close* till a boulder appears on the right, where the red *Sentier des 25 Bosses* crosses over the path to go uphill. The roof direct, right of the red arrow, is the morpho ❒ *Yogi* 7b. Higher uphill on the red path is the excellent prow of ❒ *Prouesse* 7b, which is again morpho and easier for tall folk. Left of *Yogi*, towards the *Jean des Vignes* path, is the superb prow of ❒ *Extraction Terrestre* 7a+, climbed from a sit start from the low holes to slap up and right round the prow.

Jean des Vignes

400m along the *Chemin de Jean des Vignes* path, which eventually swings right from the car park, you will come to a clearing and junctions where boulders appear on the right. There is an excellent ◆ blue circuit (D+ no. 1) well worth a visit, with 35 problems and 12 variants. Test pieces include ❒ *Simili Poutre*, a R-L 7a traverse opposite blue 6 bis and just to the right of 6 bis is a good dyno above the hole – ❒ *Coup de Vent Directe* 7a. The ❒ *Surplomb* roof on the far side of blue 7 is an excellent 7a deep sit start.

Rocher des Potêts

This quiet area of low boulders is not often visited but good for beginners. From the parking at Croix Saint-Jérôme, follow the *Jean des Vignes* path to the junction at the boulders there (400m), take a left onto the *Chemin du Rocher des Potêts*, where the ◆ orange circuit (AD no. 2, 36 problems) starts on the right after about 100m. For the ◇ yellow circuit (PD no. 1, 46 problems) continue along the path a little further, veering right at the *Vallée Close* junction, until boulders appear on the right shortly after.

Mont Pivot

One boulder in particular is worth visiting – an unusual pocketed yellow wall just under the summit ridge of Mont Pivot itself. The best way to find this is to follow the red *Sentier des 25 Bosses* from Roche aux Sabots, through the forest to cross the Mont Pivot path and uphill to the summit (15 minutes). From here, the boulder is just under the ridge on the south east side. ❒ *Pancras* is the pocketed prow at 7b+ sit start, ❒ *Belle Gueule* 7a is the high yellow pocketed wall to the left, 7b from a sit start. These problems are worth seeking out if you enjoy pocket-pulling. There are a few more problems on walls below this closer to the main paths downhill, such as the giant slab of ❒ *Le Dernier des Géants* 7a, 100m below *Belle Gueule.*

Rocher de la Justice de Chambergeot

This is a very quiet old yellow circuit area, now mostly abandoned and a little dirty and lichenous, but it has some good test pieces and some scope for new problems. It is extremely accessible to Musardière campsite and lies on a pleasant pine hilltop. It is sometimes referred to as 'Châteauveau'. The ◇ yellow/orange circuit (PD+ no. 1) has 33 problems plus 16 variants and starts downhill at the Croix Saint-Jérôme side and continues uphill, but is in need of attention, watch the landings as well. The area can be accessed on foot via the *Pommier Sauvage* path, off the Grandes Vallées road: 200m or so north of Musardière, there is a track into parking on the right side of the road from where you should follow the *Chemin de la Plaine du Pommier Sauvage* for two hundred metres – as it turns the corner to go uphill, veer off right to the EOS boulder and the main ridge boulders above. ❒ *EOS* is an excellent sit start 7b problem on the low blunt roof arête, the mantle to its left is also good: ❒ *Golden Roc* 6c. On the ridge are some large boulders round the giant *Rocher de la Justice* (with yellow 13). The prow on the roofed boulder just east of this is ❒ *Turbulence* 6c from a sit start. ❒ *Rubicube* 6c+ is the R-L traverse of the steep wall of the *Rocher de la Justice.* ❒ *Coup de Sirocco* 7a is the pillar-like arête right of the yellow arrow (left of yellow 4).

La Roche aux Oiseaux

A side-show to Roche aux Sabots, but worth it if you want some solitude and over 100 'off-piste' problems. North-west of the main Sabots car-park - from the exit circle, follow the *Chemin de la Saussaye* north for 600m. It a modest collection of boulders with a ◆ blue circuit of 37 problems and many test pieces. The sidepull wall of ❒ *Brazil* (7a) is superb, just north-east of the blue 26 & 33 blocs. The low roofed boulder in front of this has the classic scooped prow of ❒ *Le Mandarin* (8a) which requires some unusual pressing technique.

❐ Rocher du Potala

LA VALLÉE DE LA MÉE

Le Vaudoué village lies on the south-east corner of the Trois Pignons and is the base for a number of climbing areas. The main forest walk of *Le Chemin de la Vallée de la Mée* allows access to some of the most atmospheric bouldering venues in the south of the Trois Pignons. The best bouldering is found at: *Rocher Potala, J A Martin & Rocher Cailleau, Rocher Fin*, as well as at the very accessible *Rocher Guichot*.

❒ *Diplodocus*

Other areas include:

Diplodocus

This is an interesting clearing with some bizarrely-shaped giant boulders and short walls, named after the spiny dinosaur-shaped head that lies on the sand under the highest boulder. The pleasant ◇ yellow, ◆ blue and ◆ orange circuits have just over 20 problems each. To get there follow the *Vallée de la Mée* to a left turn after 700m onto the *Chemin du Rocher Fin*. The clearing and boulders are visible on the left shortly after.

Rocher du Général

This is a small area north-west of Diplodocus, continue along the path past this area to turn left onto the *Chemin de la Plaine de la Mée* and the boulders soon appear at the base of a hill on the right. The ◇ yellow circuit (PD+ no. 2) has 24 problems. The ◆ blue circuit (TD- no.1) has 41 problems and 13 variants and starts slightly further along the path. ❒ *Ictus* is a super 7a wall marked with a green arrow, found on the back of a boulder left of Blue 21 and 22.

Rocher de la Cathédrale

This is a small area before Potala on the red *Sentier des 25 Bosses*, which can be followed on the right 200m along the *Le Chemin de la Vallée de la Mée* from the forest car park at Le Vaudoué. Turn left at the *Chemin de la Cathédral* and go along this till it rejoins the red path where the boulders appear. It has a good long ◆ orange circuit (AD+ no.1) which has 55 problems and 20 variants up to 6a, most problems are 2 to 4.

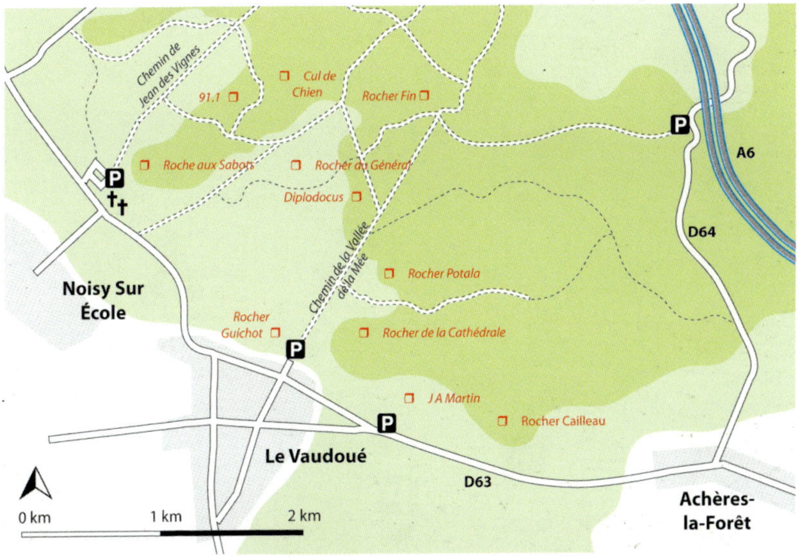

ROCHER GUICHOT

p.43

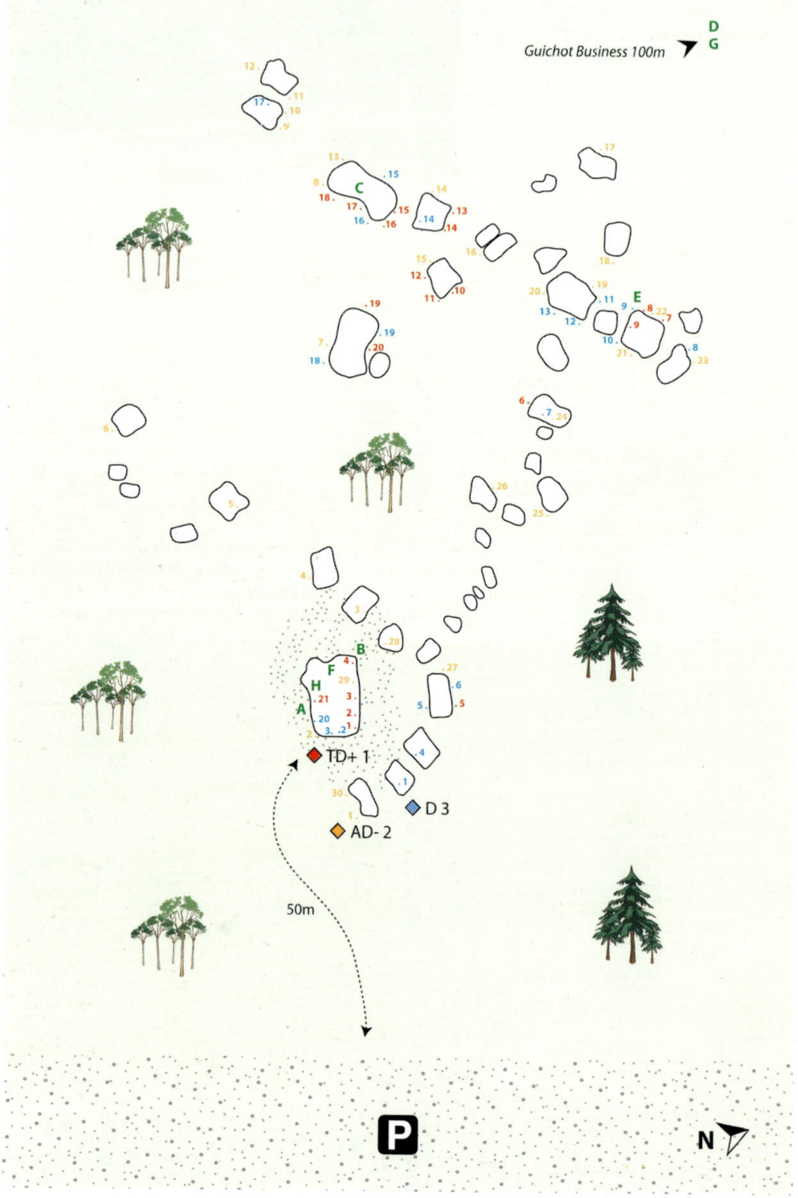

ROCHER GUICHOT

BLOC NOTES >>> Lying only 50m west of the *Vallée de la Mée* car park north of Le Vaudoué, this is a popular and compact venue, providing shade on sunny days, though it dries slowly after rain. The red circuit is excellent and worth doing as an introduction to the crimpy technicality of the forest's circuits.

CIRCUITS >>> A reworked ◆ orange circuit (AD- no. 2) has 30 problems plus 1 variant. The blue circuit ◆ (D no. 3) is a fun circuit of 20 problems. All good, try the No.3 *Fatigue* for a Font 4! ◆ The red (TD+ no. 1) circuit is a justifiably popular short circuit of 21 problems. All problems start on the first boulders just left of the car-park as you enter.

TEST PIECES >>>

❒ A. *La Verrue*	6b	Left of blue 20, this is a good dynamic direct problem.
❒ B. *Drôlesse*	6b	Red 4 slopey arête.
❒ C. *La Michetonneuse*	6c	Slopey roof direct of red 17.
❒ D. *Guichot Business*	6c+	Downhill to a roofed boulder about 100m north of blocs. Right side of prow.
❒ E. *Jour de Rêve*	7a	Left side of prow between red 8 and 9.
❒ F. *Duègne*	7b	Back roof of big boulder. Crouch start red 21 into groove.
❒ G. *Achoppement Libre*	7b	Downhill to a roofed boulder about 100m north of blocs. Left side of prow.
❒ H. *L'Atelier*	8a	Traverse blue 20 to red 21 exit.

❒ Guichot Business

❒ Red 12

❒ Red 4

❒ La Verrue

ROCHER DU POTALA

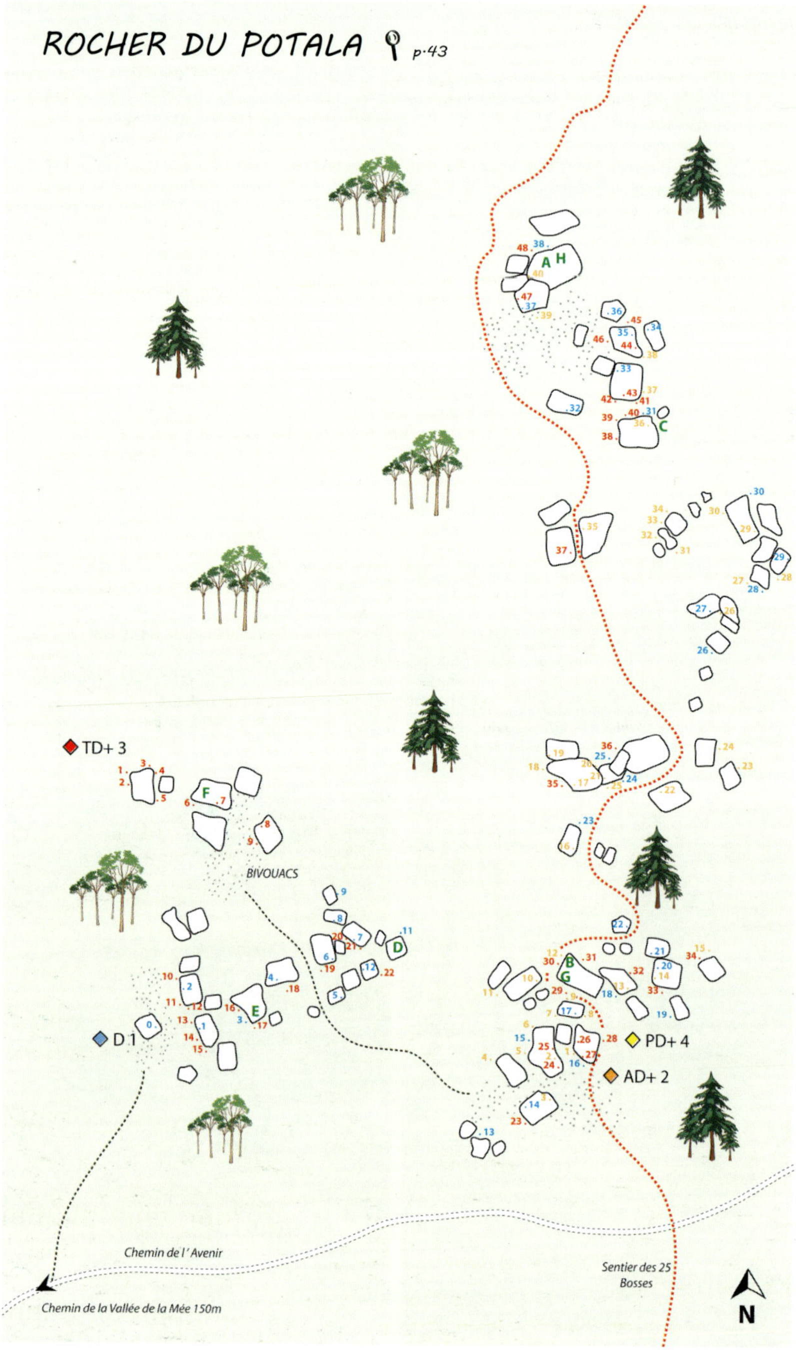

ROCHER DU POTALA

BLOC NOTES >>> Rocher du Potala is a quiet area in the south of the Trois Pignons more commonly frequented by local circuit climbers. The boulders are a delightful ochre in places and the landings are mostly flat and sandy. The circuits are really too good to be ignored, as the place does not have too many off-circuit classics, aside from the essential *Surplomb de la Vallée de la Mée* which became famous in the nineties – this 8a is a must if you are strong enough, but it's worth a look for anyone wanting to understand the level of dedication often required in the forest.

ACCESS >>> The boulders are located on a sunny south-western flank of the ridge of *Le Sentier des 25 Bosses* north of Le Vaudoué and just east of the straight path of the *Chemin de la Vallée de la Mée*. The boulders are only 20 minutes walk from Le Vaudoué, but if coming by car, drive to the Rocher Guichot car-park north of the *Rocher Cailleau* suburban road. From here walk north along the *Chemin de la Vallée de la Mée* for 500m to a crossroads, turn right onto the *Chemin de l'Avenir*, continue for 250m till the boulders appear on the left by a sandy area, where the orange circuit begins. The red and blue circuits start further west.

CIRCUITS >>> The ◇ yellow circuit (PD+ no. 4) has 36 problems and starts by the orange circuit. The ◆ orange circuit (AD+ no. 2) is superb and follows a trail of 40 problems and 8 variants. The ◆ blue circuit (D no. 1) has 38 problems and 13 variants, starting to the west of the area in an amphitheatre of boulders. One of the best circuits in the forest is the ◆ red circuit (TD+ no. 3) with 48 numbers and 9 variants, starting in the north-west 'bivouac' area and following a trail east and up the hill.

TEST PIECES >>>

❒ A. *Tortues Jumelles*	6a	The classic, puzzling last red 48 – twist and commit on the arête.
❒ B. *The Crack*	6b	Red 30. The hanging crack to the left of and above *Étrange Étrave*.
❒ C. *La Poussière qui Tue*	6c+	SS low roof, match the sloper to gain the big hole.
❒ D. *Printemps d'Automne*	7a	SS the blunt nose by Blue 11, clamp and aim up right, exit left is 6c+.
❒ E. *Samarkande*	7a+	The roof of red 17 from the right cave start.
❒ F. *La Porte du Temps*	7a+	SS low crimps left of red 6 to the horizontal crack then arête to top.
❒ G. *Étrange Étrave*	7b+	SS to red 30 through the roof, exit with crack and arête.
❒ H. *Surplomb de la Vallée*	8a	Gain high blunt undercuts left of Blue 38, break left and mantle.

❒ Potala

❒ Orange circuit

❒ Red circuit

❒ Surplomb de la Vallée

❒ Rocher Guichot

❒ Potala > Étrange Étrave

❒ Path to paradise

❒ Potala > Printemps d' Automne

❒ Follow the yellow brick road

❒ Rocher Fin landscape

❒ Rocher Fin > Le Menhir > Yellow Circuit

❒ Rocher Fin > Bras de Fer > Red 29

❒ Rocher Fin > The Cube

ROCHER FIN p.43

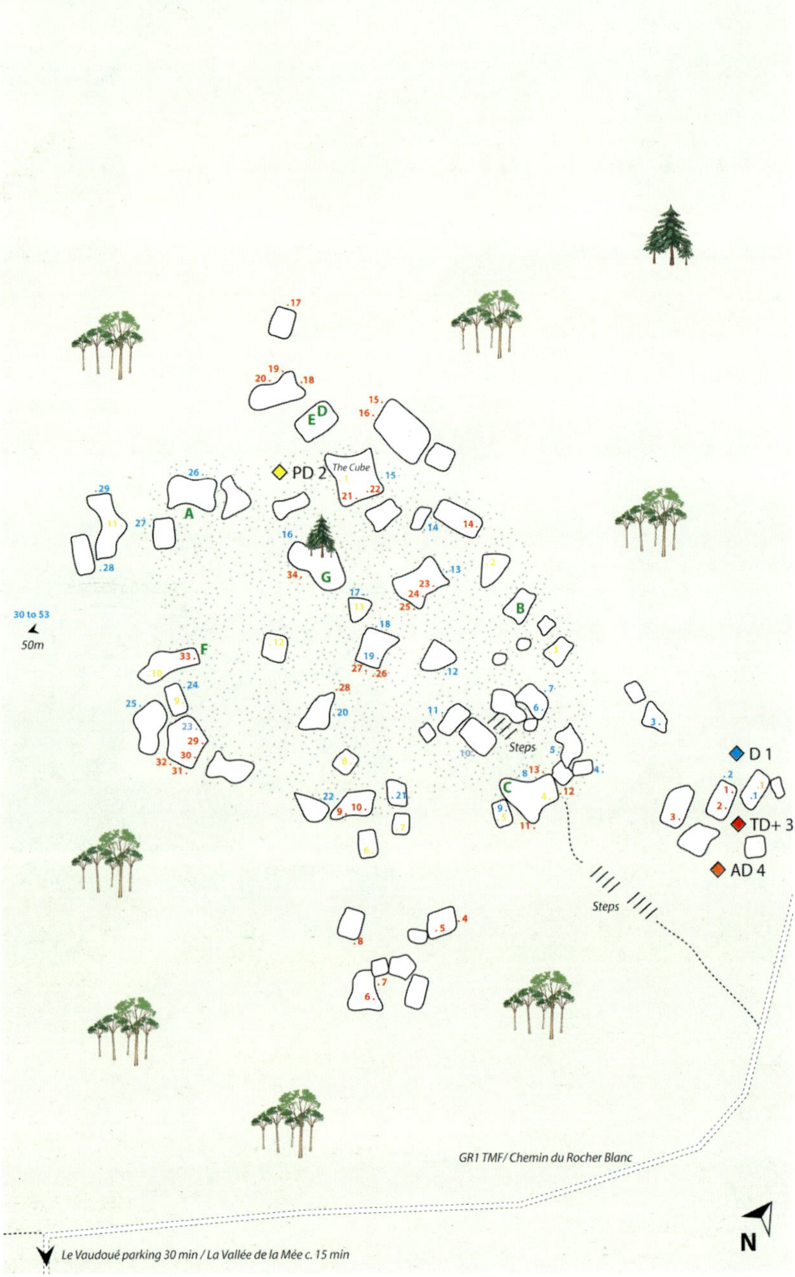

ROCHER FIN

BLOC NOTES >>> Rocher Fin is one of the more remote areas of the Trois Pignons and excellent for escaping the crowds. It's also a fine sandy exposed site, which dries very quickly after rain but can be too hot in summer. The rock is a delightful marbled ochre sandstone, often crimpy and technical on small *grattons*. The landings are good and sandy so make sure you take a bristled mat to rid your shoes of eroding sand grains. There are a number of steep roof test pieces, but it is more attractive as a fun and compact circuit venue.

ACCESS >>> Rocher Fin is best approached from the *Vallée de la Mée* car-park at Le Vaudoué. Follow the *Chemin de la Vallée de la Mee* for 1500m then turn left at a sandy area onto the *Chemin du Rocher Blanc*. From here, meander uphill through boulders onto the top of the hill where a sandy area is ringed by attractive boulders. The area can also be accessed after Diplodocus by continuing over a cross-roads and veering right along the *Chemin du Rocher Blanc*.

CIRCUITS >>> The ◇ yellow circuit (PD no. 2) has 14 problems going clockwise round the hill, best are 1, 4, 10, 13 (circuit starts in the sandy area). The ◆ orange circuit (AD no. 4) has 40 problems and 4 variants, starting in the east of the area. The ◆ blue circuit (D no. 1) has 53 good problems and 14 variants, starting in the east of the area, then meanders downhill west at the end. Try 8,15, 19, 23, 27, 38, 39, 43, 50. The ◆ red circuit (TD+ no. 3) has 34 problems and two variants, with some real crimp-fests. Go for 17, 20, 21, 23, 29, 30, 31, 32, 34.

TEST PIECES >>>

❒ A. *Ana-Krakatoa*	7a	SS volcano-shaped cave to gain crack to top.
❒ B. *Naufrage d'une Illusion*	7a	Undercut wall opposite yellow 3. Dyno or static.
❒ C. *Mémoire d'Outre Tombe*	7a+	SS low prow from deep cave, exit right on slopers and arête.
❒ D. *Les Serbes*	7a+	Opposite red 18. Wall via curved crack, no arête.
❒ E. *Les Croates*	7b	Hole and wall to right of *Les Serbes*.
❒ F. *Starting Bloc*	7c	SS red 33, climbing the steep projecting nose left.
❒ G. *Les Zinzins de l'Espace*	8a+	Traverse R-L on a beautiful marble wall to finish up red 34.

❒ Red 29

❒ *Les Zinzins de l' Espace*

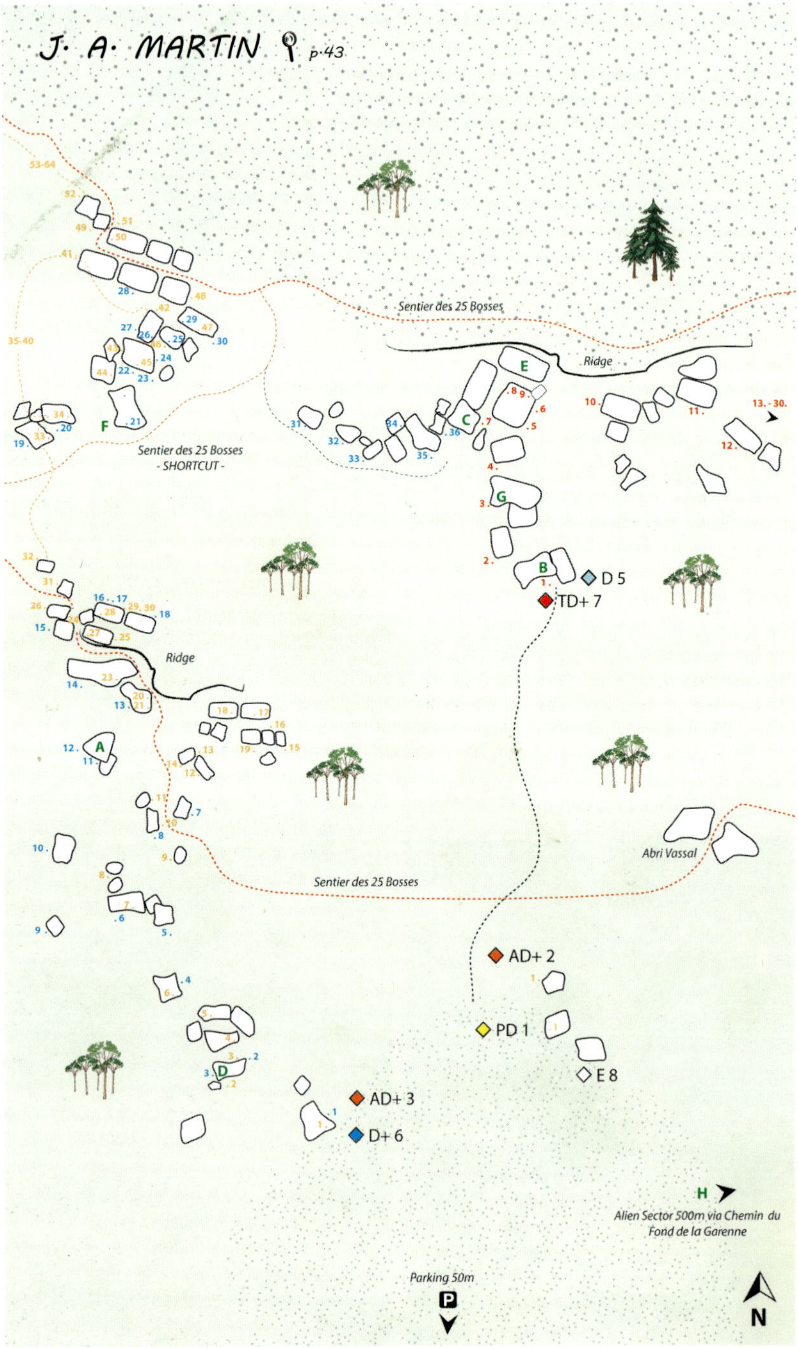
J. A. MARTIN p.43
Sentier des 25 Bosses
Ridge
Sentier des 25 Bosses
- SHORTCUT -
Ridge
Abri Vassal
Sentier des 25 Bosses
D 5
TD+ 7
AD+ 2
PD 1
E 8
AD+ 3
D+ 6
H
Alien Sector 500m via Chemin du
Fond de la Garenne
Parking 50m
N

J. A. MARTIN (ROCHER CAILLEAU)

BLOC NOTES >>> This quiet area may be a bit rambling and in some cases highball, but it has some of the forest's best problems, in particular the stunning feature that is *L'Étrave*. The problems are all on boulders on the various interlinked ridges and in the sandy bays below these ridges. The blue circuit is excellent.

ACCESS >>> 1km east of Le Vaudoué crossroads on the D63 Achères-La-Forêt road. Park in the large car-park, signposted as 'Rocher Cailleau' on the first bend in the road. From the east end of the car-park walk north to a sandy area to the start of the blue circuit on the left, leading uphill. For the red circuit, follow the central path straight uphill to the marble-spattered *Mur du Son*. *L'Étrave* is situated on the *Sentier des 25 Bosses* shortcut 'raccourci' path (dotted red marks), in a small valley on the north side of the Blue Circuit ridge. Further east along the base is a small valley where the red circuit finishes. The *Chemin du Fond de la Garenne* from the east of the parking bay leads in about 400m to the *Alien* area, follow a short uphill track on left for 50m (directly behind the 'gravures' interpretation panel).

CIRCUITS >>>
The ◇ white kids' circuits begin in the main sandy area at the base of the hill. A ◆ yellow circuit (PD- no. 1) also begins here, with 54 problems. Two orange circuits go in opposite directions from the sandy bay, the ◆ (AD+ no. 2) with 86 problems heads north-east and the ◆ (AD+ no. 3) with 64 problems and 14 variants heads north-west. The ◆ blue circuit (D+ no. 6) is a super clockwise round of 36 problems following the ridges, starting in the sandy area on the left. The ◆ sky blue circuit (D no. 5) starts up towards the ridge and has 50 problems and nine variants. The ◆ red circuit (TD+ no. 7) starts at *Le Mur du Son* and heads uphill before tracking back east downhill, it has 30 original problems reworked to 50 if you have the stamina.

TESTPIECES >>>

❒ A. *L'Arête du Marbre*	6b	Right of blue 11, this sharp arête is artful. Step on from the plinth.
❒ B. *Le Mur du Son*	6c	Red 1. Highball *gratton* wall is a classic test of nerve.
❒ C. *Le Printemps de Martin*	6c+	The zig-zag overhanging ledges left of the red 7 crack.
❒ D. *Outil de Coupe*	7a	The steep prow by blue 3 from a sit start.
❒ E. *Coup de Cymbale*	7a+	Narrow corridor wall opposite red 9, sidepulls, then a jump!
❒ F. *L'Étrave*	7b+	Climb the shapely prow, by the path, via crimp left of high arête.
❒ G. *L'Homme de Pierre*	7c	Arch roof right of red 3.
❒ H. *Alien*	7c	Big roof traverse R-L. SS right via sloping rail to central finish. Central

SS with right finish is ❒ *Coeur d'Alien* 8a. The central left sit start from the hole is ❒ *Vandale* 7c.

❒ J A Martin

❒ J. A. Martin > L' Étrave

❒ J. A. Martin > The super blue circuit

❒ J. A. Martin > Arête du Marbre

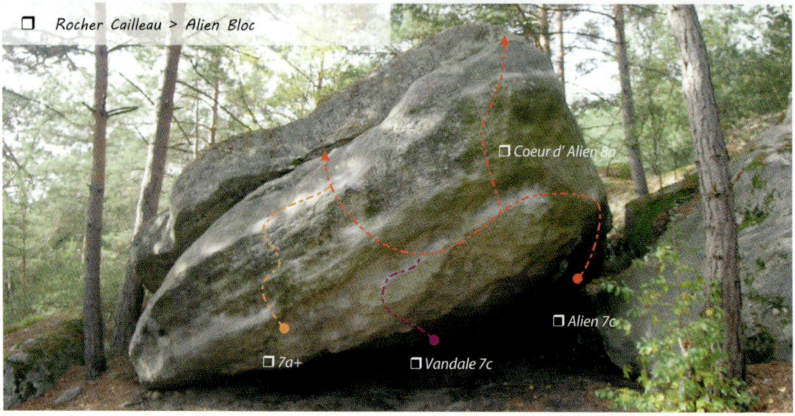

❒ Rocher Cailleau > Alien Bloc

❒ Canche aux Merciers > Le Nez

❒ Canche aux Merciers > Blue circuit

❒ Canche aux Merciers > Mardi Gras

❒ Canche aux Merciers > La Baleine

CANCHE AUX MERCIERS

p.20

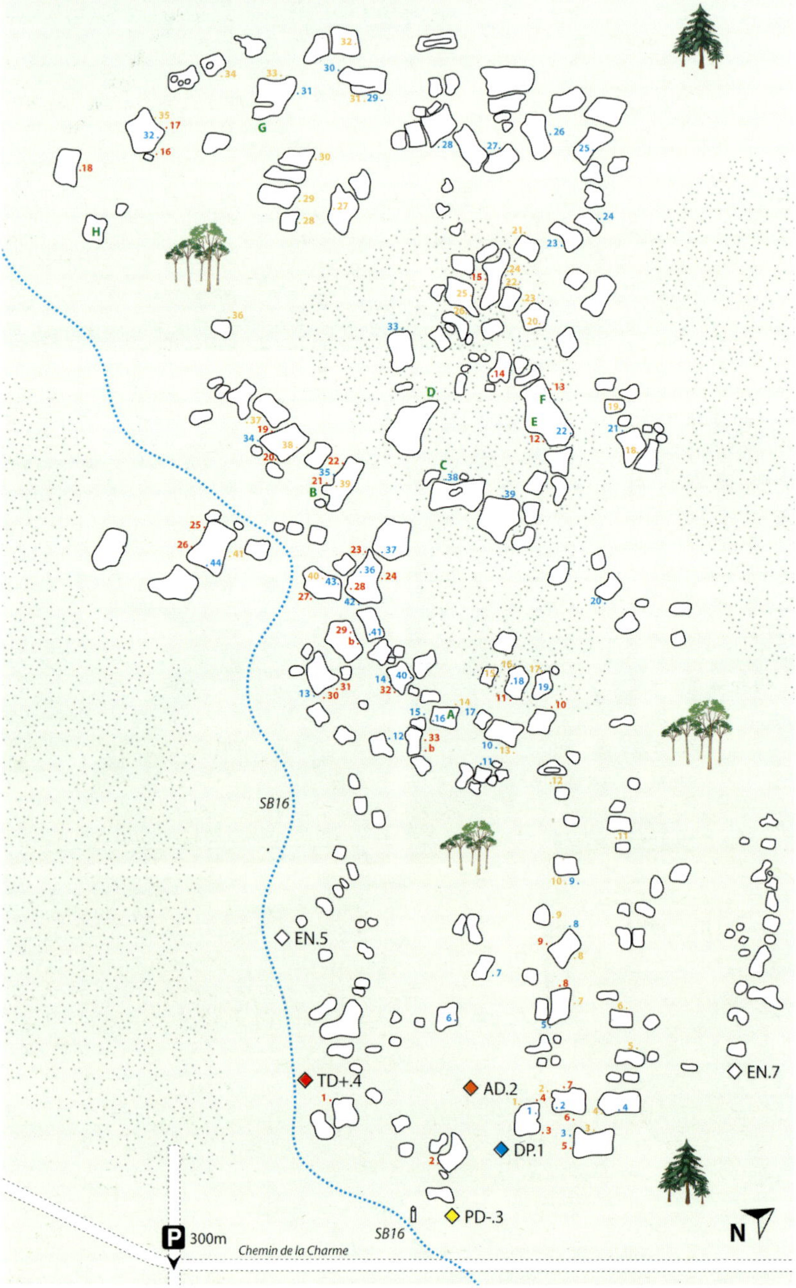

CANCHE AUX MERCIERS

BLOC NOTES >>> 'Hair-grass of the haberdashers', as it translates, 'Canche' a popular spot and a busy and compact bouldering area. The orange, blue and red circuits are excellent and there are two white kids' circuits. The slightly polished rock is often populated by children on school trips, or occasionally army cadets on training, and the motorway can add to the noise, so choose early mornings or late evenings. The boulders are generally quite low and traverses are popular. There are few test-pieces, but this laid-back venue is best for doing circuits and enjoying the sandy landings if your technique should fail! It dries quickly after rain.

ACCESS >>> As for the Bois Rond: from the roundabout at Arbonne-la-Forêt, go south and after the bend look out for a subway on the right a few hundred metres along the straight. This leads under the A6 flyover motorway to a large car-park. Take the wide sandy track leading northwest into the forest and after 300m, turn right onto the *Chemin de la Charme*. The boulders soon appear on the left, where most of the circuits begin. On the south of the path is a quieter, hardcore area on the SB16 path known as *Anarchodrôme*.

CIRCUITS >>> Two ◇ white kids' circuits (EN nos. 5 & 7) start from either side of the boulderfield, stringing together an enjoyable playtime for beginners. The ◆ yellow circuit (PD- no. 3) is a faded long meander, perhaps surpassed by the ◆ orange circuit (AD no. 2) which is enjoyably technical and climbs some attractive features. The ◆ blue circuit (D+ no. 1) has 45 crimpy and technical traverses and a variety of problems on walls, roofs and arêtes, highlights being 8, 10, 11, 16, 22, 28, 34, 35 and 44. A discretionary 45th problem can be found in the concrete crack under the flyover! The ◆ red circuit (TD+ no. 4) is another classic crimp-fest with 33 problems thrown in and seven harder variant problems. Highlights on this superb circuit are: 6, 9, 11, 13, 14, 15, 16, 22 and 32. There are not too many classic straight-ups, as most problems can be made harder by traverses.

TEST PIECES >>>

❒ A. *Kéo*	7a	A double dyno between crack and sidepulls on the back of blue 16.
❒ B. *Mardi Gras*	7a	Sit start arête on dinosaur skin finishing right of or up red 21.
❒ C. *Gros Doigts*	7a	A stretchy sit start to blue 38 from the flake crimps.
❒ D. *Le Nez*	6b+	The low pocketed roof is always chalked, mantle out.
❒ E. *Rage Dedans*	7b+	The deep dark roof left of red 12.
❒ F. *La Puce*	8a	Full-body dyno under roof to lip of red 13.
❒ G. *La Baleine*	7a	Whale lip R-L traverse, finish direct (7a+) or up arête.
❒ H. *Parafine*	7a	L-R traverse of low boulder via crimps to right arête.

❒ Red 22

❒ Red 1 © Stuart Stronach

❒ Blue circuit

❐ Bois Rond > La Théorie des Nuages

❐ Bois Rond > Toubib or Not Toubib

❐ Bois Rond > Orange Circuit

❐ Bois Rond > Blue Circuit

❐ Bois Rond > Red Circuit

❐ Drei Zinnen > Multipass Wall

❐ Drei Zinnen > Close Contact

❐ Drei Zinnen > Bifurcation

❐ Rocher de la Reine

❐ Chemin du Bois Rond > 3 venues

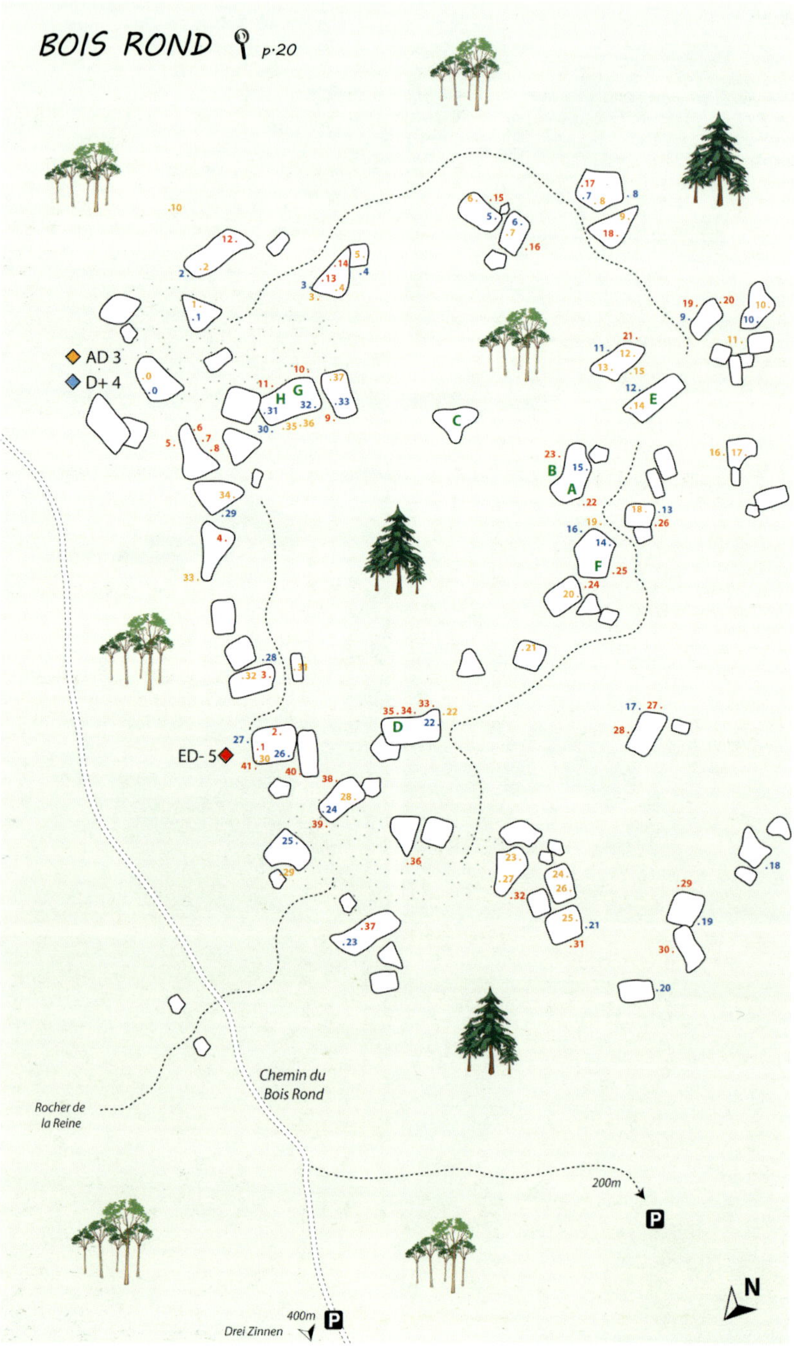
BOIS ROND
p.20
AD 3
D+ 4
ED- 5
A
B
C
D
E
F
G
H
Chemin du Bois Rond
Rocher de la Reine
200m
P
400m
Drei Zinnen
N

BOIS ROND

BLOC NOTES >>> The Bois Rond is exactly that - a 'round wood', with a series of circuits in a tranquil and compact situation amongst tall trees. The orange, blue and red circuits provide some classic problems. The harder test pieces are powerful but not highball. It is worth trying some of the famous traverses such as *Galalactique* or *Le Tourniquet*. This is a good quiet area away from the crowds at Canche Aux Merciers and just below the ridge areas of Drei Zinnen and Rocher de la Reine, should you wish to explore further. The real test piece is *Lucky Luke,* done by Marc Le Menestrel in 1993.

ACCESS >>> The Bois Rond is five minutes east from the small car-park opposite the Canche aux Merciers entrance (about two kilometres south of the Arbonne-la-Forêt roundabout on the D64), just after the bend car-park for Drei Zinnen. Walk into the woods along a rough track till you hit the *Chemin du Bois Rond*, turn right and follow this for 150m metres until the boulders appear on the right, just a few metres into the woods. Alternatively, park carefully at the wee bend car-park as for Drei Zinnen and head east along the *Chemin du Bois Rond* until the blocs appear on the right. Rocher de la Reine is just opposite up the hill.

CIRCUITS >>> The ◆ orange circuit (AD no. 3) is a fun round of 37 steady problems plus 11 variants, try 1, 9, 14, 17, 22 bis, 35. The ◆ blue circuit (D+ no. 4) is one of the hardest to getting going on, you'll find out why ... it has 33 problems plus 2 variants, try classic 'stoppers' such as 1, 2, 5, 13, 19, 24, 27, 28. The ◆ red circuit (ED- no. 5) is a super and hard circuit of 40 clockwise problems with 17 variants. Go for 6, 10, 14, 17, 23, 24, 25, 35, 37, plus the must-do red 22! For some reason red 22s in the forest are always classics, this may be entirely coincidental, or some sort of Bleausard conspiracy of excellence.

TEST PIECES >>>

❒ A. *Le Meilleur des Mondes*	6a	Red 22. A real puzzler to start, and the pocketed seam above is technical.
❒ B. *La Théorie des Nuages dir.*	6b	Sit start left of red 23 and climb roof direct.
❒ C. *La Quille*	6b	SS the 'cobra' prow exiting right. Left var. through slopers is 7a.
❒ D. *Constellation d' Amoureux*	6c+	Red 35. From hole, traverse left to mantle into the groove.
❒ E. *Le Tourniquet*	7a	Girdle traverse round Orange 14 boulder, using lip holds and wall.
❒ F. *Toubib Or Not Toubib*	7a	Red 24 bis. Gain slopey left hand sidepull and dyno to top.
❒ G. *Sensation*	7b+	Dyno between red 10 and 11 to top from slopers in horizontal seam.
❒ H. *Lucky Luke*	7c	Crimpy wall just right of red 10 and left of *Sensation*.

❒ Red 13

❒ Lucky Luke wall

❒ Red 22

DREI ZINNEN

p.20

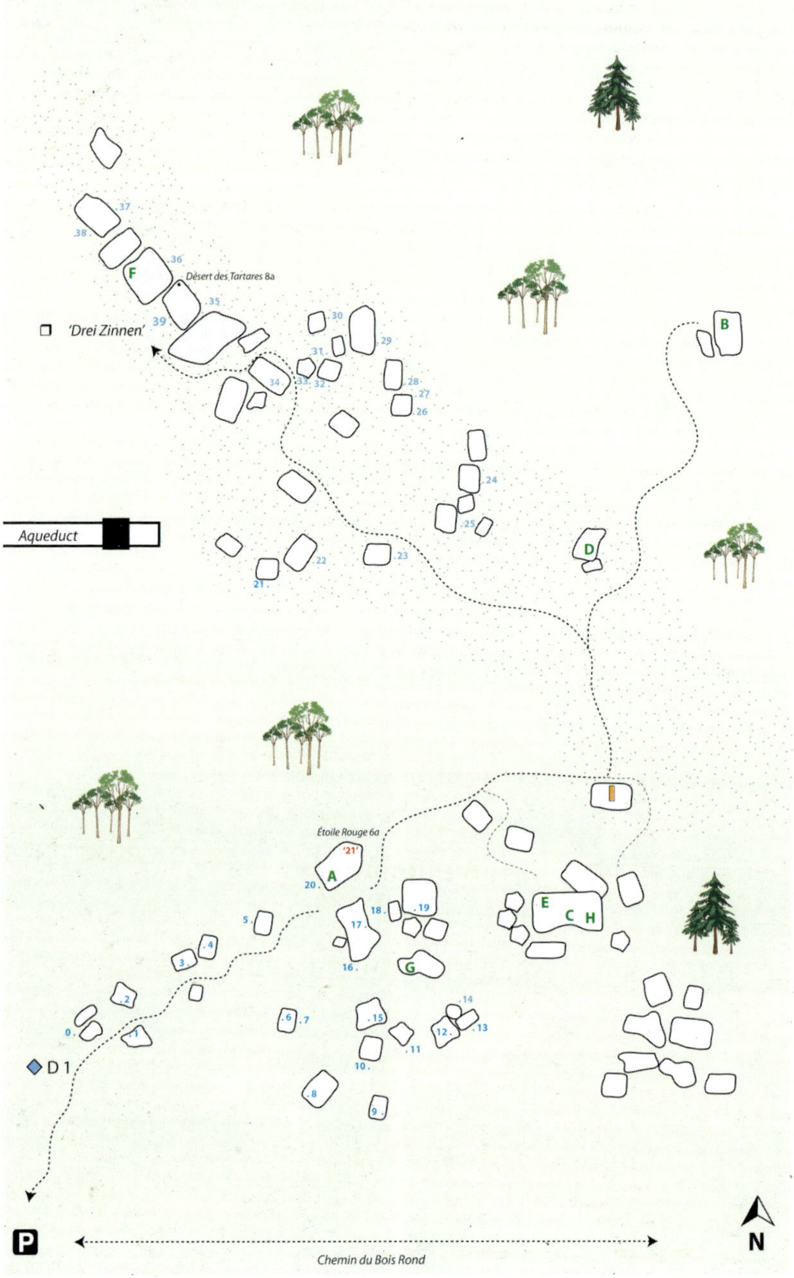

DREI ZINNEN

BLOC NOTES >>> The *Drei Zinnen* (3 Towers), is an original hardcore venue, where some truly stunning and highball lines were created in the 90s. That said, there are some modern lower classics from 7a and above. The blue circuit is also worthwhile. The area is never very busy as most people visit the more popular Canche aux Merciers, but if you are feeling strong, it is a must-visit venue. The motorway is noisy and can distract a little, but the rock is quality and hours will be lost here to complex and difficult sequences.

ACCESS >>> The Drei Zinnen ridge, with its Waterboard aqueduct, lies two kilometres south of the *Arbonne -la-Forêt* roundabout, on the D64, just east of a blind bend. Drive south from the roundabout signed for *Achères-la-Forêt* until the road turns the left bend onto a straight. Slow down here and park in a layby on the corner by the start of the *Chemin du Bois Rond,* easy to miss as the road straightens – watch out for traffic when entering or leaving! The Bois Rond car-park is a little further on the left side, you can park here and walk back if the spot is taken. For Drei Zinnen, walk directly uphill towards the aqueduct and veer right for the start of the blue circuit and *Sale Coup* area. For the *Multipass* area, go to the top of the hill and the distinctive 'Drei Zinnen' boulders.

CIRCUITS >>> The ◆ blue circuit (D no. 1) at Drei Zinnen has 39 problems heading uphill with 16 variants.

TEST PIECES >>>

❒ A. *Sale Coup*	7a	SS the cracked cave right of Blue 20 and climb the crack via underclings.
❒ B. *Ordalie*	7a+	The marbled roofed wall. SS at edges and twist your way to the lip jugs.
❒ C. *La Fosse aux Oreilles*	7b	SS left cave and exit to the right via undercling. 6c var. to right.
❒ D. *Pantoum*	7b	Roof problem from flake crack in cave out to slopers then a crimpy finish.
❒ E. *Diversion*	7b	SS cave at low right pinch, through pocketed overhang, finishing right.
❒ F. *Multipass*	7b	Left arête of tower wall. Starting from right is the harder *Matière Grise 7c.*
❒ G. *Close Contact*	7b+	Slopey roofed arête. SS low up to right arête, left to crux sloper finish.
❒ H. *Cocoon*	7c	Rounded arête right of *La Fosse aux Oreilles*.

❒ *Diversion*

❒ *Diversion Roof*

❒ *Fosse aux Oreilles*

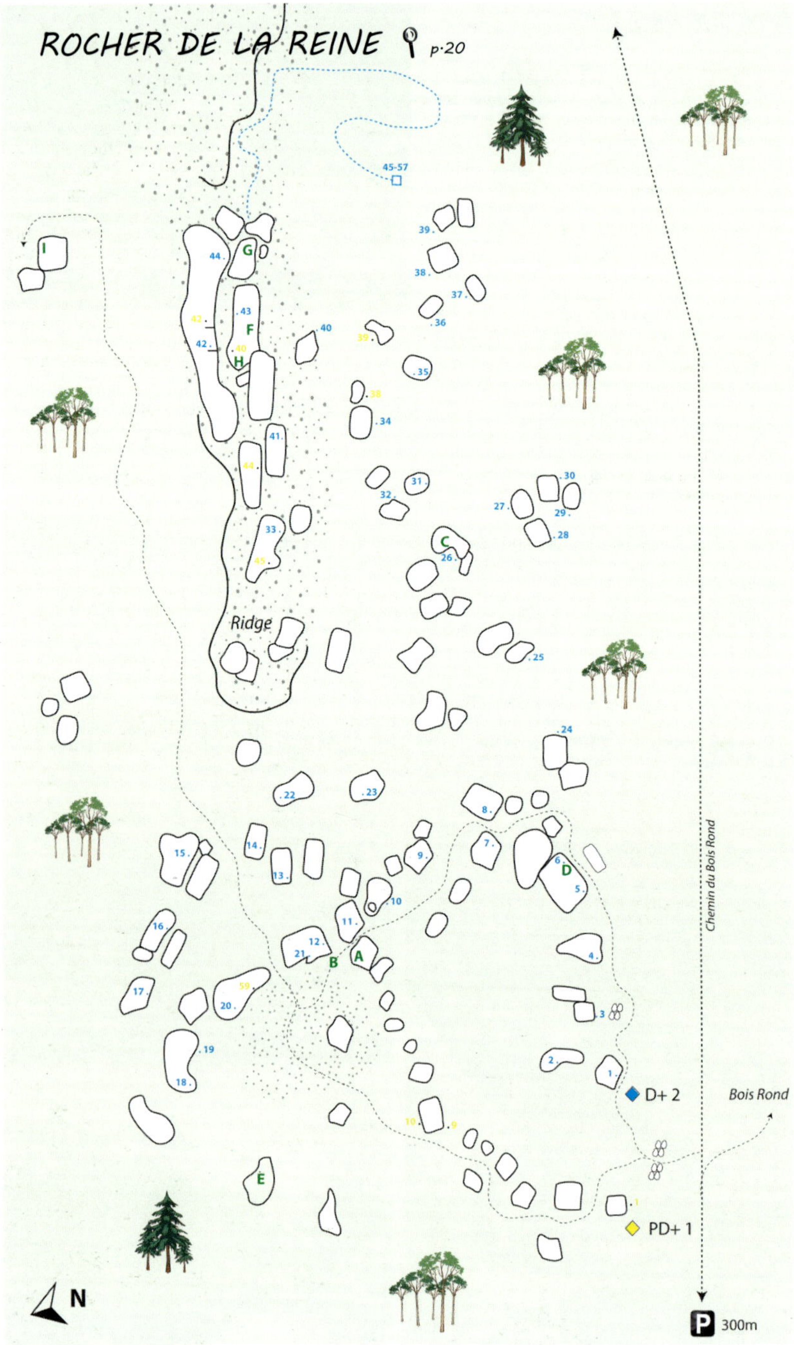
ROCHER DE LA REINE
p.20
45-57
Ridge
Chemin du Bois Rond
Bois Rond
D+ 2
PD+ 1
300m
N
A
B
C
D
E
F
G
H
I

ROCHER DE LA REINE

BLOC NOTES >>> 'The Queen's Rocks' is really a continuation of the *Drei Zinnen* ridge, but is somewhat less intense in ambience with lower walls and blocs and a pleasant secluded feel for working shorter projects. The boulders lie on a hillside and the landings are generally okay, though some have tree roots and awkward blocs so a large mat is useful. The split nature of the ridge allows problems on both sides of the ridge and in hidden canyons and pits, so it is quite a complex area to get to know. The ridge continues for some way tracing blue and yellow circuits. Most problems lie on the southern flank blocs so it is a sunny spot.

ACCESS >>> Park at the *Bois Rond* car-park opposite *Canche aux Merciers*. Take the path into the woods until it meets the *Chemin du Bois Rond*, turn right and 100m later the rocks appear on the left opposite the Bois Rond rocks. For the main blocs, head uphill via the yellow circuit to the ridge.

CIRCUITS >>> The ◆ blue circuit (D+ no. 2) has 57 problems heading uphill on the right from the path, with 12 variants. The ◇ yellow circuit (PD+ no. 1) starts on the left of the path and has 59 problems.

TEST PIECES >>>

❐ A. *Napoleon*	6a	Short prow wall via pockets and slopers to apex. SS from sidepulls is 7a.
❐ B. *Plumes aux Ventes*	6b	Leaning arête right of blue 21 to a mantle finish. SS is 7a.
❐ C. *Newton*	6c	SS cave into blue 26.
❐ D. *Ramapithèque*	6c+	SS wall just left of blue 6. Traverse from Blue 5 is 7a+ *Jules Verne*.
❐ E. *SR71*	6c+	SS slopey north scoop of small bloc 15m left of blue 18.
❐ F. *La Porte du Temps*	7a	The layback flake crack and slopey mantle behind tree on yellow 40 wall.
❐ G. *Couguar Blanc*	7a	SS right of blue arrow and go left to hole then direct up via pocket.
❐ H. *Compression Zip*	7a+	SS out of cave by yellow 40 to clamp up slopey prow.
❐ I. *Hotline*	7c	Giant arête, north and downhill of ridge, via a vague path right of Blue 15.

❐ *Newton*

❐ *SR71*

❐ *Ramapithèque*

❐ *Hotline*

FRANCHARD ISATIS

p·67

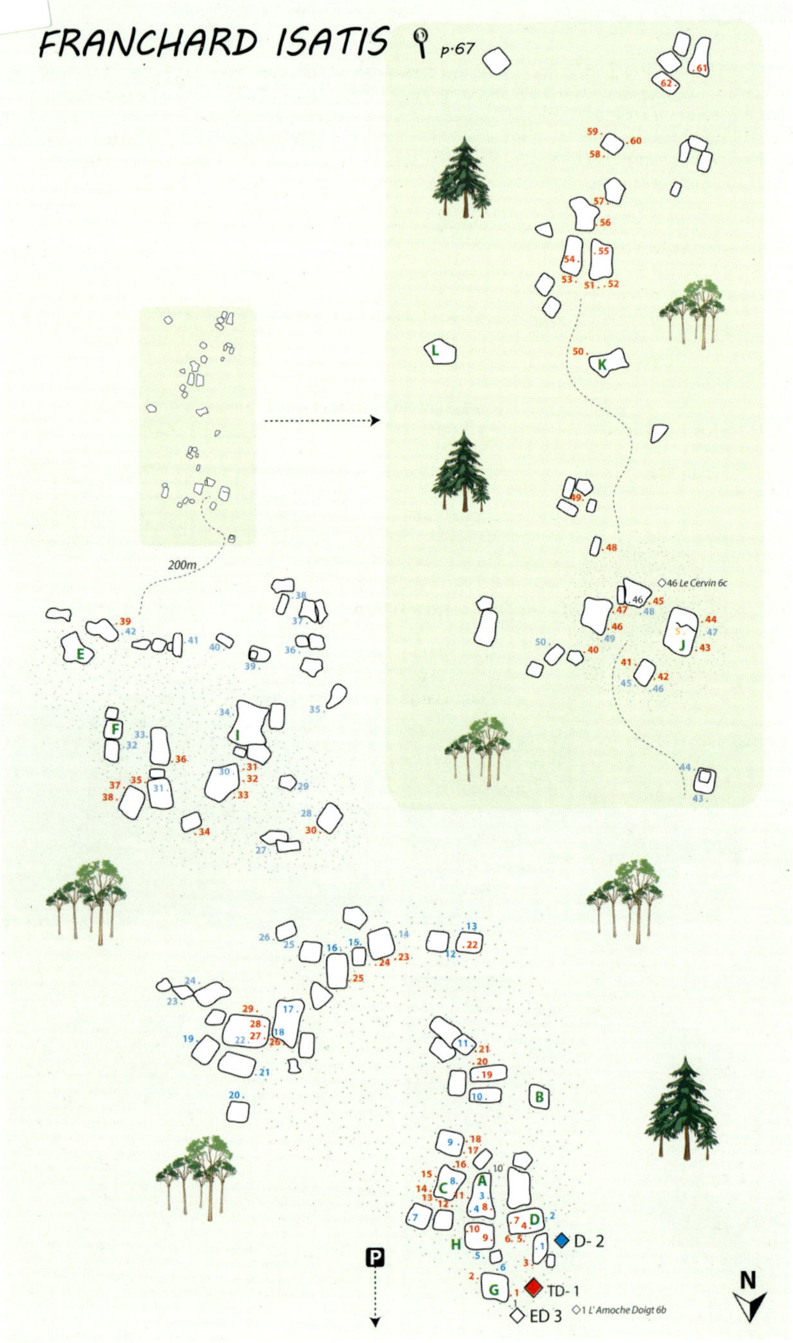

FRANCHARD ISATIS

BLOC NOTES >>> This superb shaded forest area has hundreds of boulders on low plains and on blunt ridges along the famous walkways of the *Gorges de Franchard*. There are a number of remoter areas, but easily the most popular are *Isatis* and *Cuisinière*, and the backwoods areas of *Hautes Plaines* and *Sablons*, all of which lie just south of the very straight D409 between Fontainebleau and Arbonne-la-Forêt. After rain, the boulders are slow to dry but on a cool sunny day with the breeze in the pines, this is perfection – there are unlimited good problems at all grades, making this one of the must-visit areas of the forest. The circuits are excellent, with some real classics amongst them, and the tree-cover allows shady conditions and often cool mornings.

ACCESS >>> 2km east of Arbonne-la-Forêt. The access is on the south side of the road about half way along the straight.. Watch out for red and white marker posts on the south of the road which is the *Route du Loup* track leading to the *Isatis* parking a few hundred metres along a gravel track. From the parking here, Isatis is 50m south into the woods. A wide track *Route de l' Isatis* leads east to the ridge area of *Cuisinière.*

CIRCUITS >>> Isatis has four classic circuits: the ◆ orange circuit (AD no. 4) has 45 problems and 11 variants, starting deep in the woods south of the *Routes des Gorges de Franchard* at the south end of where all the other circuits end. The ◆ blue circuit (D- no. 2) starts in the main parking area and heads south up the blunt ridge of blocs, with 50 fun problems and 7 variants. The ◆ red circuit (TD- no. 1) is a classic with 63 problems entwining with the blue circuit, a long journey of perfection. The ◇ white circuit (ED no. 3) is a Bleausard education, with 50 problems and 2 variants, mainly between 5+ and 6c, it's hard and very long. Starts at the *Sur-prises* boulder (the first bloc from the parking), essentials: 3, 4, 10, 16, 19, 24, 29, 32, 35, 40, 46, 50.

TEST PIECES >>>

❒ A. *Le Surplomb Statique*	6a+	White 10. The slopey roof through boss from standing. 7c+ sit start.
❒ B. *La Beurre Marge*	6b	White 16. A scooped wall, made of buttered slopers.
❒ C. *L' Envie des Bêtes*	6b+	The undercut marbled wall left of red 14 is a little masterpiece.
❒ D. *Composition des Forces*	6c	White 4. A superb fingery undercut direct up to a sloper finish.
❒ E. *El Poussah*	7a	Hanging prow, jump from pocket through slopers, toe-hook!
❒ F. *L'Angle Ben's*	7a+	Very square arête on smears, steep side of white 40.
❒ G. *Sur-prises*	7b+	First bloc classic - undercling to high right scoop, mantle.
❒ H. *Le Mur des Lamentations*	7b+	A beautiful technical wall, the finest in the forest, travel up and left.
❒ I. *Alta*	7c	Right of blue 34, the bulge via undercut sidepulls to a slopey top.
❒ J. *La Memel*	7b	Giant boulder's marbled and blunt arête.
❒ K. *Iceberg*	7a+	The floating prow via slopers on right. Sit start is 7b+, traverse L-R 8a.
❒ L. *L'Insoutenable...*	8b	'Unbearable lightness of being' required to escape this roof.

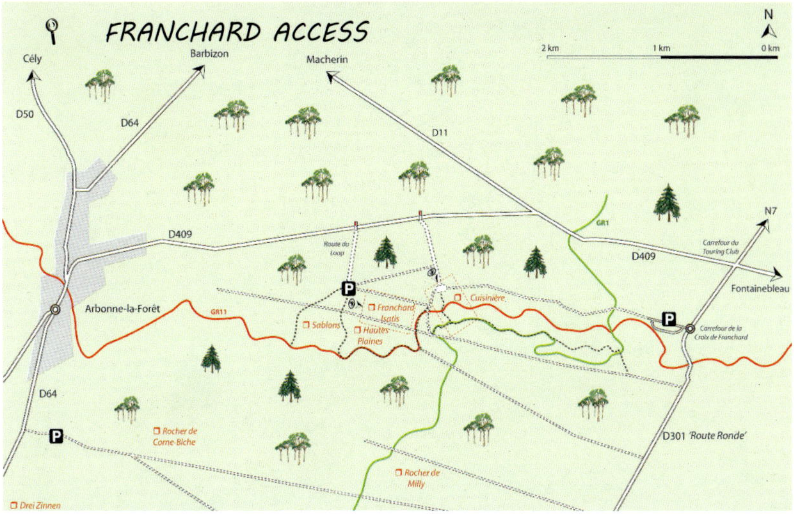

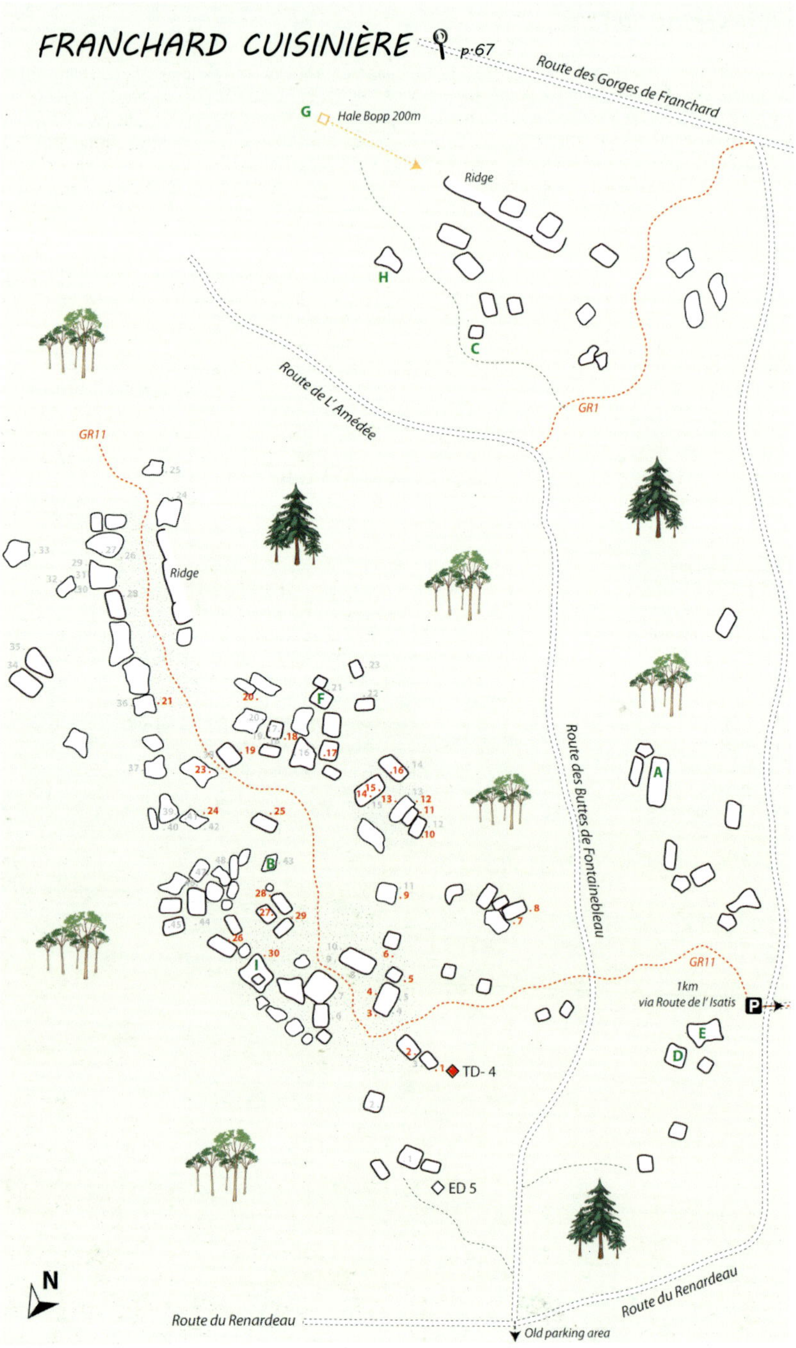
FRANCHARD CUISINIÈRE
p.67
Route des Gorges de Franchard
G
Hale Bopp 200m
Ridge
H
C
Route de L'Amédée
GR1
GR11
Ridge
F
A
Route des Buttes de Fontainebleau
B
I
GR11
1km
via Route de l' Isatis
P
E
D
TD- 4
ED 5
N
Route du Renardeau
Route du Renardeau
Old parking area

FRANCHARD CUISINIÈRE

BLOC NOTES >>> The 'pressure-cooker' of hard test pieces. This is a heavily wooded area which is slow to dry and green after rain, but in dry conditions it is one of the classic areas of the forest with hundreds of fine boulders. It's probably most famous for its white circuit and for the desperate test pieces such as the fingernail slab of *Duel* 8a, as well as the awe-inspiring *Karma 8a+*. There are classic problems at all grades though access is now further west at *Isatis*. Most problems are accessed via the central *Route des Buttes* and lie amongst the hillside jumbles of boulders. As it is so complex, look out for the biggest boulders and find a reference point such as a white circuit number.

ACCESS >>> As for the *Isatis* parking, a few hundred metres south on a gravel track from the D409. From the parking, head east along a wide track *Route de l' Isatis* for 1km to turn left at the *Route du Renardeau* which bends round to the old parking area under the ridges of *Cuisinière*. From the clearing, the *Routes des Buttes* goes south into the forest, veer immediately left into the woods to the red and white circuit areas on the left hand hillside, or right to the classic *Excalibur* and the old black circuit area on the right hill. To access the clean-cut dyno wall of *Hale Bopp*, walk east along the ridge from the *Duel* area for 200m along the orange mountain circuit – you'll find boiler-plate walls facing south over the *Route des Gorges des Franchards*.

CIRCUITS >>> Cuisinière has two ◆ orange circuits, the short one in the main area (AD+ no. 1) has 18 problems, and a wandering, easy 'mountain circuit' – a 5 km scrambling circuit, follow the orange double dashes up the ridge from the *Route Amédée*. The ◆ red circuit (TD- no. 4) has 31 problems entwining with the white circuit, uphill on the left from the *Routes des Buttes*. The superb ◇ white circuit (ED no. 5) climbs the left ridge from the same area and has 48 problems , from 4 to 6b, with 13 marked variants to 7a.

TEST PIECES >>>

❐ A. *Moondance*	6a	Old black 8. A central left line of the big vertical wall.
❐ B. *Mathusalem*	6b	The scooped ledge and wall just left of the direct 7a *Le Mur Cordier*.
❐ C. *De Fil en Aiguille*	6c	Clean arête and cross-crack wall left of GR1 path (50m right of *Duel*).
❐ D. *Excalibur*	7a	Blunt arête left or right at the top – both finishes hard and reachy!
❐ E. *Beatle Juice*	7a+	SS pocketed overhang opposite *Excalibur* from far left to right.
❐ F. *Haute Tension*	7b	Crimpy wall right of white 21 – a Jacky Godoffe tester.
❐ G. *Hale Bopp*	7c	Morpho dyno wall. From crimps launch to the top!
❐ H. *Duel*	8a	Classic fingernail slab. Most walk on by…
❐ I. *Karma*	8a(+)	Jump pit roof to finger-jugs and beg onto the slab right of red 30.

❐ *Excalibur*

❐ *Duel*

❐ *Karma*

❐ Franchard Isatis > Blue Circuit

❐ La Coquille > Photo © Sean Bell Photography

❐ Isatis > Mur des Lamentations

❐ Isatis > Alta

❐ Isatis > Le Statique

FRANCHARD SABLONS & HAUTES-PLAINES

BLOC NOTES >>> These backwoods area of Franchard have a couple of quieter circuits and solitude for test pieces, situated on the south side of the main arterial path of the *Route des Gorges de Franchard*. There are many classic hidden test piece problems worth researching in depth before a visit. Very much a 'lost-in-the-forest' atmosphere which was famous because of *Millenium* for a time.

ACCESS >>> As for the *Isatis* parking. For *Hautes-Plaines*, take the *Route du Loup* (west side of parking) south to a crossroads on the *Route des Gorges de Franchard*. Continue on ahead along a path to where the yellow circuits start on each side of path. For *Sablons*, follow the *Route du Cul de Chaudron* to a crossroads, circuits on the left shortly after.

CIRCUITS >>> *Sablons* has two circuits, the ◆ red circuit (TD no. 1) with 26 problems and a ◆ blue circuit (D no. 4) of 35 problems and 8 variants. *Hautes-Plaines* has two ◇ yellow circuits: (PD no. 2) of 21 problems and (PD+ no. 3) of 25 problems and 6 variants, as well as an ◆ orange circuit (AD+ no. 5) of 43 problems and 9 variants.

TEST PIECES >>>

❒ A. *Modulor*	7b+	Bear-hug prow in corridor, opposite blue 12. (Sablons)
❒ B. *Le Surplomb de la Coquille*	6c	Hidden prow/wall underneath yellow 10 in pit. (Hautes Plaines)
❒ C. *Le Solitaire*	7a	Leaning prow, on slope above path under yellow circuit ridge.
❒ D. *Lapin ou Canard*	7a	SS overhang to slopey prow, exit right by perched bloc of yellow 25.
❒ E. *Cœur Bondissant*	7a	SS marbled overhang opposite yellow 5 across path.
❒ F. *Le Mur Lombard*	7a	Technical vertical wall on yellow 22 boulder.
❒ G. *Jambe de Bois*	7b	SS overhang to right of yellow 4 to patina crimps, exit via undercling.
❒ H. *L'Âge d'Or*	7b+	SS short prow opposite yellow 10, just right of tree. 7b stand.
❒ I. *Millenium*	8a	Roof under yellow 24, by path. Gain central lip from left, mantle.

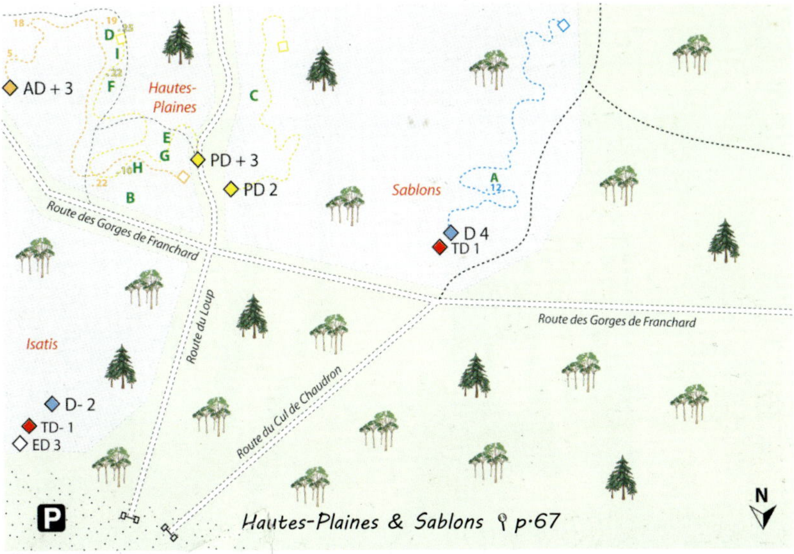

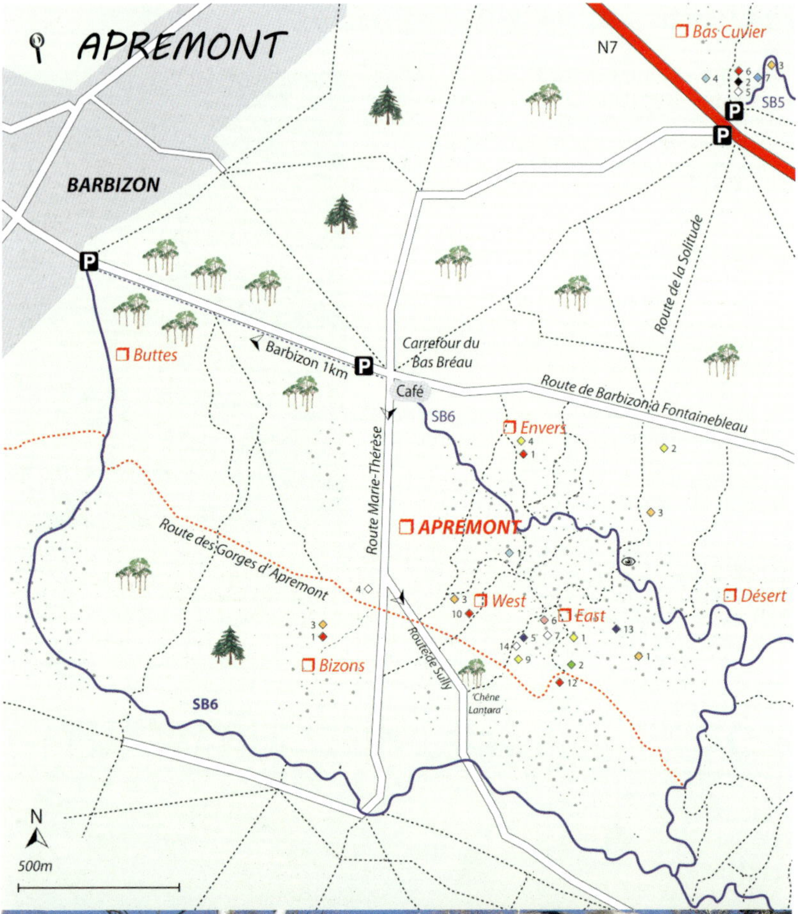
APREMONT
BARBIZON
N7
Bas Cuvier
SB5
Route de la Solitude
Carrefour du Bas Bréau
Barbizon 1km
Café
Buttes
SB6
Route de Barbizon à Fontainebleau
Envers
Route Marie-Thérèse
APREMONT
Route des Gorges d'Apremont
West
East
Désert
Bizons
Route de Sully
'Chêne Lantara'
SB6
N
500m

APREMONT

BLOC NOTES >>> Apremont is the vast and beautiful bouldering ground east of the bustling painters' village of Barbizon. There are many good areas in the sandy gorges and on the plateaux, all accessed from the 'Bas Bréau' crossroads. The character of the area is one of a painter's colourful palette: ochres and tans, greys and greens, with the complex mazes of boulders allowing you to get lost in its vast tranquillity. The main 'chemins' such as the *Route de la Solitude* and the *Route de Sully* allow access to these areas with some hidden test pieces and some classic circuits such as the Salmon circuit at Apremont Gorges (East). Sunny and quick drying.

ACCESS >>> Make your way into Barbizon and follow the one-way village system east to the obvious long boulevard into the forest. After 1km the road ends at a cafe at the *Bas Bréau* crossroads. For the main areas walk along the *Route Marie Thérèse* south (right) past the cafe for a few hundred metres, swinging left at a junction. The first old sandy area on the left (*Route du Dormoir*) leads to 'Apremont West'. The next sandy area (old car-parks now sealed off) leads to 'Apremont East' from the old oak of the 'Chêne Lantara'. All have paths running through them uphill to the plateau.

CIRCUITS >>> Apremont has many circuits in each discreet area, with some famous circuits such as the Salmon circuit and the 1957 classic 'crushed strawberry' circuit. The circuits tend to meander uphill from a low start by an access path.

❒ Apremont > La Lune

❒ Apremont > Hyperplomb 7a > Photo © Arran Curran

❒ *Apremont > La Balafre slab*

❒ *Apremont > Clin d' Oeil*

❒ *Apremont East*

❒ *Concept*

❒ *Science Friction*

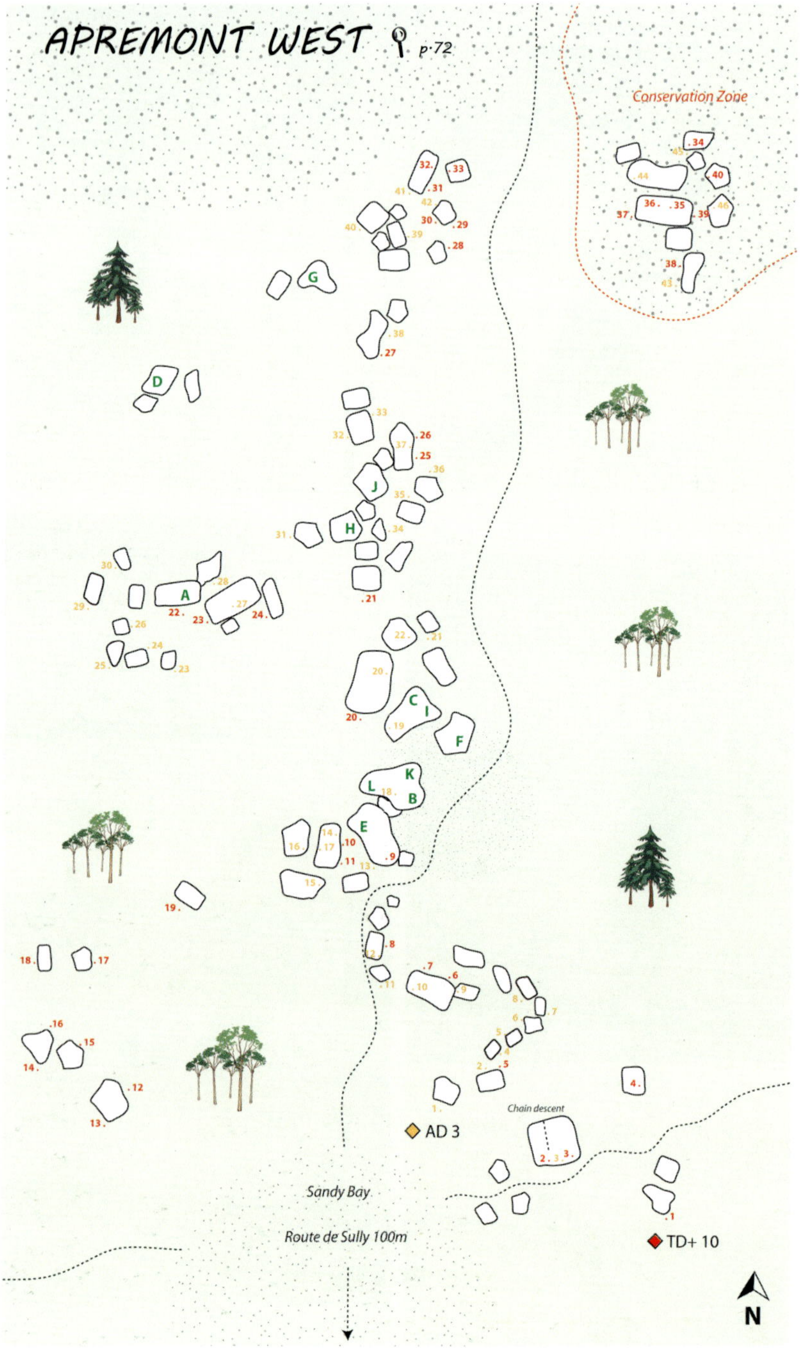
APREMONT WEST
p.72
Conservation Zone
Chain descent
AD 3
TD+ 10
Sandy Bay
Route de Sully 100m
N

APREMONT WEST

BLOC NOTES >>> Apremont West is the first main area on the left up from the *Route de Sully* and is often fairly quiet despite being accessible. A string of boulders meanders uphill from the start of the red circuit on a large boulder with a descent chain. There are a number of low powerful roof problems and a few highball testers as well, plus some desperate slab classics.

ACCESS >>> Make your way into Barbizon and follow the one-way village system east to the obvious long boulevard into the forest. After 1km park as close as you can to the cafe at the *Bas Bréau* crossroads. For the main areas walk along the *Route Marie Thérèse* south (right) past the cafe for 400 metres, swinging left at a junction onto the *Route de Sully*. The first old sandy area on the left (*Route du Dormoir*) leads to 'Apremont West'. The boulders start where a path begins to climb uphill to the plateau.

CIRCUITS >>> The ◆ orange circuit (AD no. 3) has 46 problems and 8 variants. Starts at low blocs and heads uphill. The ◆ red circuit (TD+ no. 10) has 40 problems and starts just east of a high bloc on the right with a chain descent, the problems on this are highball.

TEST PIECES >>>

❐ A. *Le Glaive*	6b	Red 22. An undercut wall then surmount lip.
❐ B. *Concept*	6c+	Cracked overhanging groove to mantle, various sequences.
❐ C. *Partie d' Échecs*	7a	Slab to right of orange 19 by tree. Left line by hole is 7b+ *Jolie Môme*.
❐ D. *Le Menhir*	7a	High pillar 50m above red 22. Trend left from right arête.
❐ E. *Super Stalingrad*	7a	Highball wall to the left of red 9.
❐ F. *Hiéroglyphes*	7a+	Blunt arête up from *Concept*. Right start needs a cheat stone or mats.
❐ G. *Crazy Horse*	7b	Low roof high on the ridge, SS right and gain barndoor crack on left.
❐ H. *Haka*	7b	SS low in red cave at undercling and arête, dyno up right to mantle.
❐ I. *Jolie Môme*	7b+	The slab right of hole and left of *Partie d' Échecs*.
❐ J. *Sitting Bull*	7c	Yellow roof behind wall of red 26. SS low cave and exit right.
❐ K. *Orphéon*	8a	R-L low traverse through holes to finish in groove right of *Concept*.
❐ L. *Merry Christmas*	8a	SS wall through underclings left of orange 18.

❐ Concept Bloc

❐ Sitting Bull

❐ Crazy Horse

❐ Slab Testers

APREMONT EAST

p.72

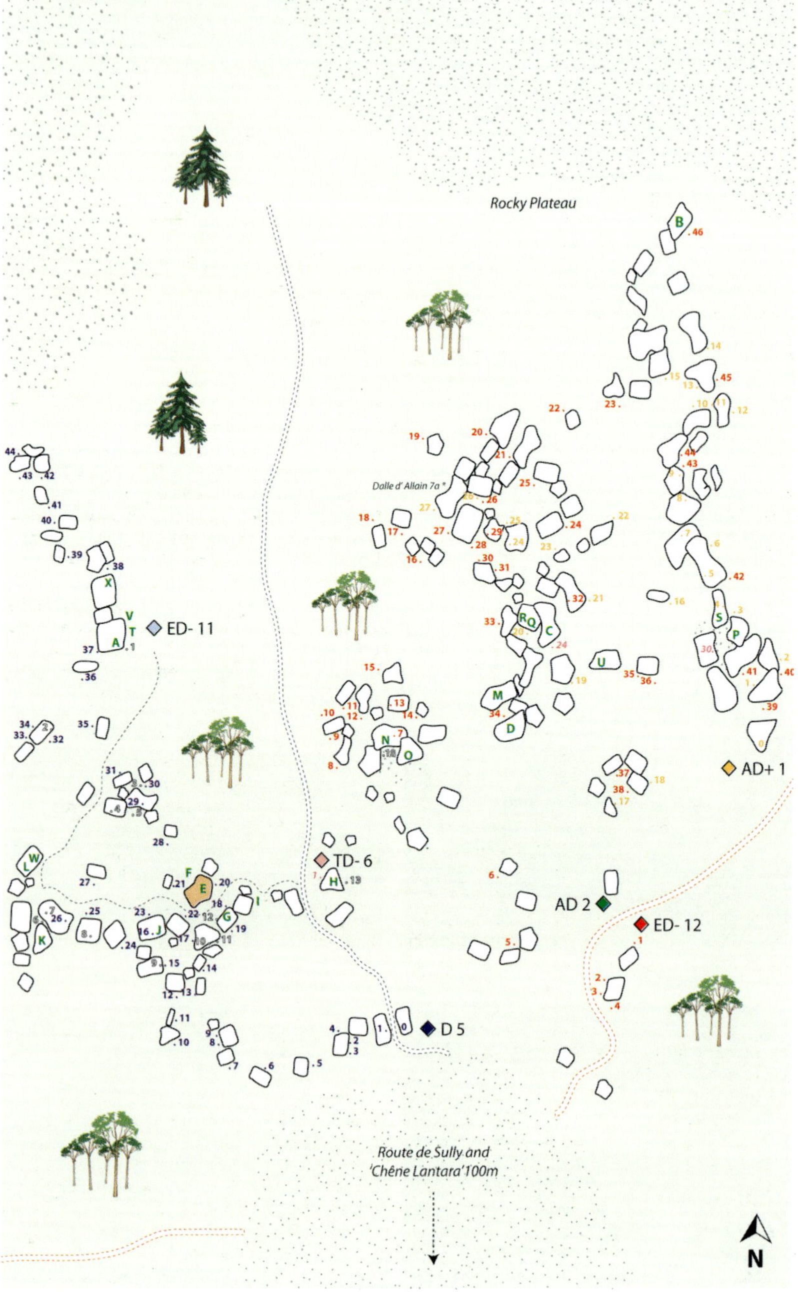

APREMONT EAST

❒ Ultramarine 20

BLOC NOTES >>> Apremont East is the second main area on the left along the *Route de Sully* above the trail of the *Route des Gorges d' Apremont* and straddles two sides of a plateau path. It has a high concentration of classic circuits and stand-out boulders.

ACCESS >>> Follow the *Route Marie Thérèse* south (right) past the cafe for a few hundred metres, veering left at a junction onto the *Route de Sully*. The first old sandy area on the left (*Route du Dormoir*) leads to Apremont West. Continue on to the large oak of the 'Chêne Lantara', then turn left to a clearing. From here a plateau path heads left and uphill between corridor blocs which mark the start of the 'Ultramarine' circuit and the heart of this sector, and the *Gorges d' Apremont* path on the right leads to the red circuit.

CIRCUITS >>> The circuits tend to meander uphill from a low start by an access path. The ◇ yellow circuit (PD+ no. 9) has 43 easy problems for beginners and starts east of the sandy area along the path of the *Routes des Gorges d' Apremont*. The ◆ orange circuit (AD+ no. 1) has 28 problems and 2 variants, starting in the far east of the low boulder jumble further along the same path. The ◆ ultramarine circuit (D no. 5) has 44 uphill problems starting at the rock corridor on the uphill path. The famous ◆ salmon circuit (TD- no. 6) is a long alpine circuit of 74 problems, heading east from the uphill path by *L'Égoiste*. The ◆ light blue circuit (D+ no. 13) is a circuit of 39 + 5 variants. The ◆ sky blue circuit (ED- no. 11) is a hard and high circuit heading downhill from the central area, with 36 + 9 variants. The ◆ red circuit (ED- no. 12) starts just along the bend in the *Routes des Gorges* path and has 46 + 5 variants. The ◇ black & white circuit (ED+ no. 7) in the east area is a classic hard collection of 14 + 2 problems with a Bleausard entry level of around 6c. The ◆ 'crushed strawberry' circuit from 1957 (D+ no. 4) has 32 classics and 8 variants and starts high on the plateau in the far east area, walk along the *Routes des Gorges* and turn left up to the top of the hill on the *Route de la Solitude*.

TEST PIECES >>>

❒ A. *L' Esprit du Continent*	5+	Sky Blue 1 is a classic highball and a test of nerve and technique.
❒ B. *La John Gill*	6a	The last in the red circuit, a roof in honour of an American guru.
❒ C. *La Balafre*	6a	Salmon 24, gain the niche and trend left to a high top with crux.
❒ D. *Science Friction*	6a	Right of red 34, smear up the slab to high right pocket.
❒ E. *Ju Jitsu*	6b	The steep ochre roof through slopers from undercling, left of blue 20.
❒ F. *Jérémiades*	6c	Back of blue 20, a vertical crimpy wall, SS is 7a+, right link 7b.
❒ G. *Lamentations*	6c+	Sky blue 12. Crimpy cracked slab to sloper up left, right var. 7a.
❒ H. *Égoïste*	7a	Slopey arête just right of path, usually chalked, SS is 7a+.
❒ I. *Clin d' Oeil*	7a	Slopey and crimpy blunt arête just left of path opposite *Égoïste*.
❒ J. *Adrénaline*	7a	Sky blue 9 bis. Easy to ledge, highball press and mantle to top.
❒ K. *Happy Boulder*	7a+	SS round bulge pit boulder left of sky-blue 8.
❒ L. *Faux Contact*	7a+	Jump-start into scooped groove and mantle out.
❒ M. *La Lune*	7a	Eliminate wall opposite red 34, no hold up left, direct to moon hold.
❒ N. *Hyper Plomb*	7a	White 1, direct wall through undercuts to slopey top.
❒ O. *La Médaille en Chocolat*	7a	White 2. Slab direct to boss. Left of salmon 13.
❒ P. *La Fosse*	7a	Leaning wall in sandpit via pocket jam to slopey top.
❒ Q. *13ème Travail d'Hercule*	7a+	White 9. Roof via foot jam, start with foot on white circle.
❒ R. *Fil à Tordre*	7a+	Left arête on boulder with *13ème Travail*.
❒ S. *Onde de Choc*	7b	The blunt prow in the sandpit area, slopey. Opposite Salmon 30.
❒ T. *Idée en l'Air*	7b	The high leaning wall right of sky blue 1. Lots of pads and spotters.
❒ U. *Tarpé Diem*	7b+	Pinches and slopers up arête left of salmon 28.
❒ V. *Psychose*	7c	The high leaning arête right of sky blue 1 and *Idée en l'Air*.
❒ W. *Full Contact*	7c+	Undercling up left into scoop of *Faux Contact*.
❒ X. *Marginal*	7c	The right arête on bloc right of *Psychose*, hard left to mantle at top.

❒ Apremont Désert > Rock sculpture

❒ Apremont Envers > Clandestino

❒ Apremont backwoods

❒ Envers > La Fissure des Alpinistes > 5+

❒ Apremont Bizons > Kids' blocs

APREMONT OTHER AREAS

BLOC NOTES >>> Apremont has a significant cluster of smaller areas around the main ridges, often with isolated test piece boulders and older circuits. They are worth exploring if you find other areas too busy, in the hot sun, or if you feel like a little solitude, an exploratory walk on featured trails, or a little nature-spotting.

ACCESS >>> *Apremont Buttes aux Peintres* is rarely frequented, but is very accessible above the 'busts of the painters' Millet and Rousseau at the exit of Barbizon and just past the night club. *Apremont Bizons* is a recently rediscovered venue of accessible blocs in the woods just south (right) of the *Route Marie Thérèse*, 200m after the junction with the *Route de Sully*. It has a kids' ◇ white circuit (EN no. 4), an ◆ orange circuit (AD+ no. 3), a ◆ blue circuit (D no. 2) of 36 + 9 problems and a good ◆ red circuit (TD no. 1) of 43 + 18 problems.

Apremont Envers is an area of hidden test pieces (such as Fred Nicole's famous roof 8b *La Pierre Philosophale*) and has a famous old ◆ red circuit (TD no. 1) of 50 plus 20 variants. There is also a ◇ yellow circuit (PD no. 4). From the cafe, take the main line east (the *Route de Barbizon à Fontainebleau*) then turn right at the *Route du Dormoir* where boulders appear uphill on the left all the way to the *Route de la Solitude* path at the east end. Continuing further along the main *Route de Barbizon à Fontainebleau* to the Félix-Herbet crossroads, leads right on the *Route de la Solitude* to a ◇ yellow circuit (PD no. 2) and an ◆ orange circuit (AD no. 3) higher uphill on the GR6. Just by the crossroads on the left of the *Route de la Solitude* is a low roof boulder with *Clandestino* etc. There is a famous Pierre Allain 5+ pillar crack called *La Fissure des Alpinistes* on the *Route du Désert* path in the eastern sector.

Apremont Désert is a remoter and ranging venue at the far end of the plateau, accessed by following the *Route de Barbizon à Fontainebleau* for 2km or so to turn south on the *Route de Clair Bois*. The boulders and a ◇ yellow circuit (PD+ no. 1) appear on the left after 200m, and a ◆ blue circuit (D+ no. 6) and an ◆ orange circuit (AD no. 4) begin together on the left a few hundred metres further along the *Route de Clair Bois*.

TEST PIECES >>>

❐ A. *Dominum*	7b	*Apremont Bizons*	Sit start to red 10.
❐ B. *Shoot*	7c+	*Apremont Bizons*	100m above orange 8. SS overhang to crimp to top.
❐ C. *La Cave Nicolas*	7a	*Apremont Bizons*	Crimpy wall left of red 15.
❐ D. *La Pierre Philosophale*	8b	*Apremont Envers*	Cracked roof from a sit start under red 43 bis.
❐ E. *Extra Balle*	7b+	*Envers/Solitude*	Right of orange 10, a rounded ball of slopey rock.
❐ F. *Clandestino*	7b	*Envers/Solitude*	The left roof direct through slopey holds.
❐ G. *El Paso*	7c+	*Envers/Solitude*	*Clandestino* but finish low right to other roof.
❐ H. *Le Pilier du Désert*	7c+	*Apremont Désert*	Large prow via jump to scoop. Right of yellow 11.

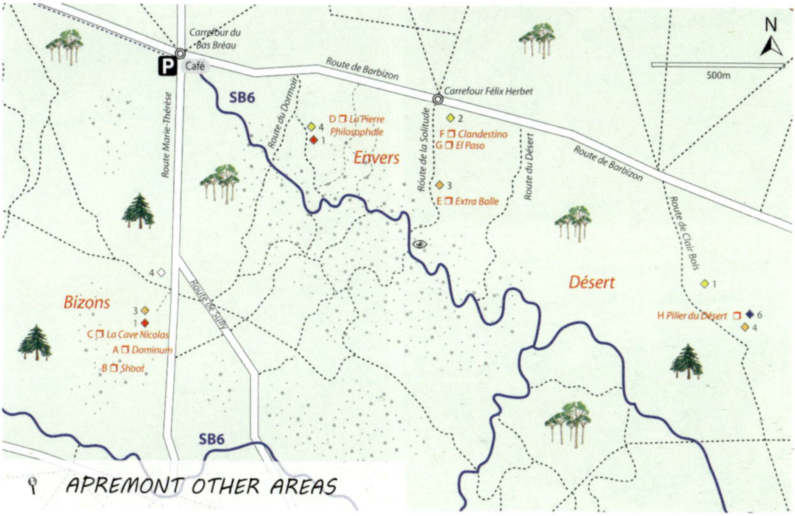

❒ Bas Cuvier > La Joker

❒ Bas Cuvier > La Balance

❒ Cuvier > Cortomaltèse

❒ Cuvier > Red Circuit

❒ Cuvier Rempart > Duroxmanie

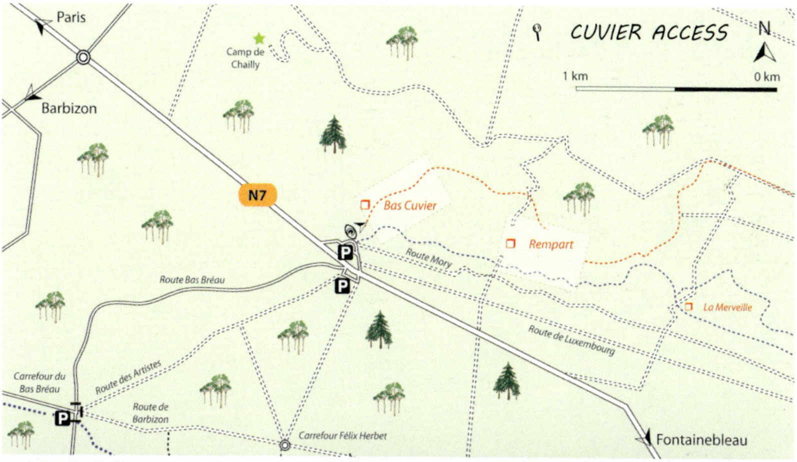

❐ Cuvier Rempart > Fourmis Rouges > Photo © Sean Bell Photography

BAS CUVIER
p.83
Route de la Solitude
Route du Sanglier
'Place Morin'
'Place du Cuvier'
AD+.3
13-30
◇ED+.5
◆ED-.2
◆TD+.6
◆TD-.7
Sentier Bleu 5
Route Mory
Cuvier Rempart
P
N

BAS CUVIER

BLOC NOTES >>> By far the most popular and historic of bouldering areas in Fontainebleau, 'Cuvier' is a system of low ridges to the east of the pretty artists' village of Barbizon and north-west of Fontainebleau. Bisected by the busy N7 road, accessibility means these areas can be busy, especially at weekends, though solitude can be found in the remote 'Rempart' south-east of the main area of 'Bas Cuvier'. This is a must-visit area and the haunt of *Bleausards*. The classics are still possible in the right cool and dry conditions, but if you are trying to crack grades, choose your time and problem with weather in mind. Bas Cuvier has thousands of problems and some classic circuits on the boulders strung along the north side of the *Sentier Denecourt 5* (blue-marked path) and the *Route de la Solitude* (red, white and green marker). Cuvier is the perfect place to start your Fontainebleau journey – just don't be arrogant and drop your grade expectations radically, for an education in the art begins here. Try the famous *La Marie-Rose* problem, or just try and complete any of the circuits and you'll begin to understand the Bleausard level of commitment and high standard of technique required to climb at Fontainebleau.

ACCESS >>> Bas Cuvier lies just beside the large car-park on the N7, 2 km south of the Barbizon turn-off, or 5 km north of Fontainebleau. Parking on both sides of the road is linked by a subway. The blue, red and white circuits all start 50m east of the east car-park. For the problems in the *Place Morin* area, such as *Carnage*, follow the red-marked *Route de la Solitude* for 150m to the sandy area on the right. For the *Marie Rose* and *Prestat* area, it's best to follow the blue-marked *Sentier Denecourt 5* through boulders to a sandy bay – it's usually busy.

CIRCUITS >>>

◆ Orange circuit (AD+ no. 3) has 50 problems but is polished. *Place du Cuvier* on the left, 50m on the SB5.
◆ Blue circuit (TD- no. 7) has 48 delightful problems, plus 4 variants. Starts opposite main parking bloc.
◇ Blue 'Philou' circuit (TD- no. 4) has 56 problems. Starts on a boulder to the left of the parking.
◆ Blue 'Pascal Meyer' circuit (D- no. 1) has 26 problems. Starts opposite *La Prestat* crack of orange 50.
◆ Red circuit (TD+ no. 6) is a classic of 42 puzzlers, the record for which is 18 minutes. Start at parking bloc.
◆ Black circuit (ED- no. 2) is an eastwards trail of 30 (+3 var.) Problems, 5 to 6c+, though number 6 is 7b.
◇ White circuit (ED+ no. 5) is a Bleausard classic of 17 test pieces and 10 variants. Start at parking bloc.

TEST PIECES >>>

❒ A. *La Prestat*	3+	Orange 50. The classic highball crack.
❒ B. *La Paillon Directe*	4+	Sky-blue 48. On the south wall of the Prestat bloc. A snaking crack.
❒ C. *L'Envers du Un*	5+	The first red circuit problem is a classic intro to Fontainebleau.
❒ D. *La Marie Rose*	6a	Red 22, first 6a in Font – a famous wall via sidepulls & slopers.
❒ E. *Erectissima*	6a+	Black 8. Superb wall and arête right of red 12.
❒ F. *La Stalingrad*	6b	White 15. High slabby wall left of orange 50 crack.
❒ G. *Pause Café*	6b+	Left side of arête, left of white 12 slab and *Fissure de la Place du Cuvier*.
❒ H. *Coup de Sang*	6c	Arête left of orange 32.
❒ I. *Cortomaltèse*	6c+	Sloper bulge just right of *Carnage* bloc to reluctant high holds.
❒ J. *La Charcuterie*	6c+	White 4. Classic undercut problem up and right. 7a without jug.
❒ K. *La Joker*	7a	White 13. Back of red 22 bloc. Undercut to crossover sequence.
❒ L. *La Super Forge*	7a	White 8. Direct slab on crimps without crack.
❒ M. *La Vie d'Ange*	7a	White 10. Technical slabby wall direct, right of blue 18.
❒ N. *Abattoir*	7a+	White 6 bis, originally 7a. Overhanging groove through blunt holds.
❒ O. *L'Angle Incarné*	7b	White 4 bis. Right of blue 9 chimney. Overlap just left of *Charcuterie*.
❒ P. *Biceps Mou*	7b	Black 6 roof. Climb the central overhang.
❒ Q. *La Dragon*	7b	L-R traverse past red 39 to finish via slopers far right.
❒ R. *Aerodynamite*	7b+	Bulging arête dyno left of red 4 from pockets to slopers.
❒ S. *La Super Prestat*	7b+	White 17. High crimpy slab right of Orange 50 crack.
❒ T. *Le Carnage*	7b+	White 6 ter. Jump to crimp, power up to slopers, trend left.
❒ U. *La Bérézina/L'Abbé Résina*	7c	White 6 quat. Slopey right to left into *Carnage*. High right toe-hook.
❒ V. *Hypothèse*	7c+	Slopey classic wall from cheatstone, left of blue 9.
❒ W. *La Balance*	7c+	Slopey prow on back of *Carnage* bloc.
❒ X. *Neverland*	8a	Undercut slopey wave roof, uphill north 70m above white 2.

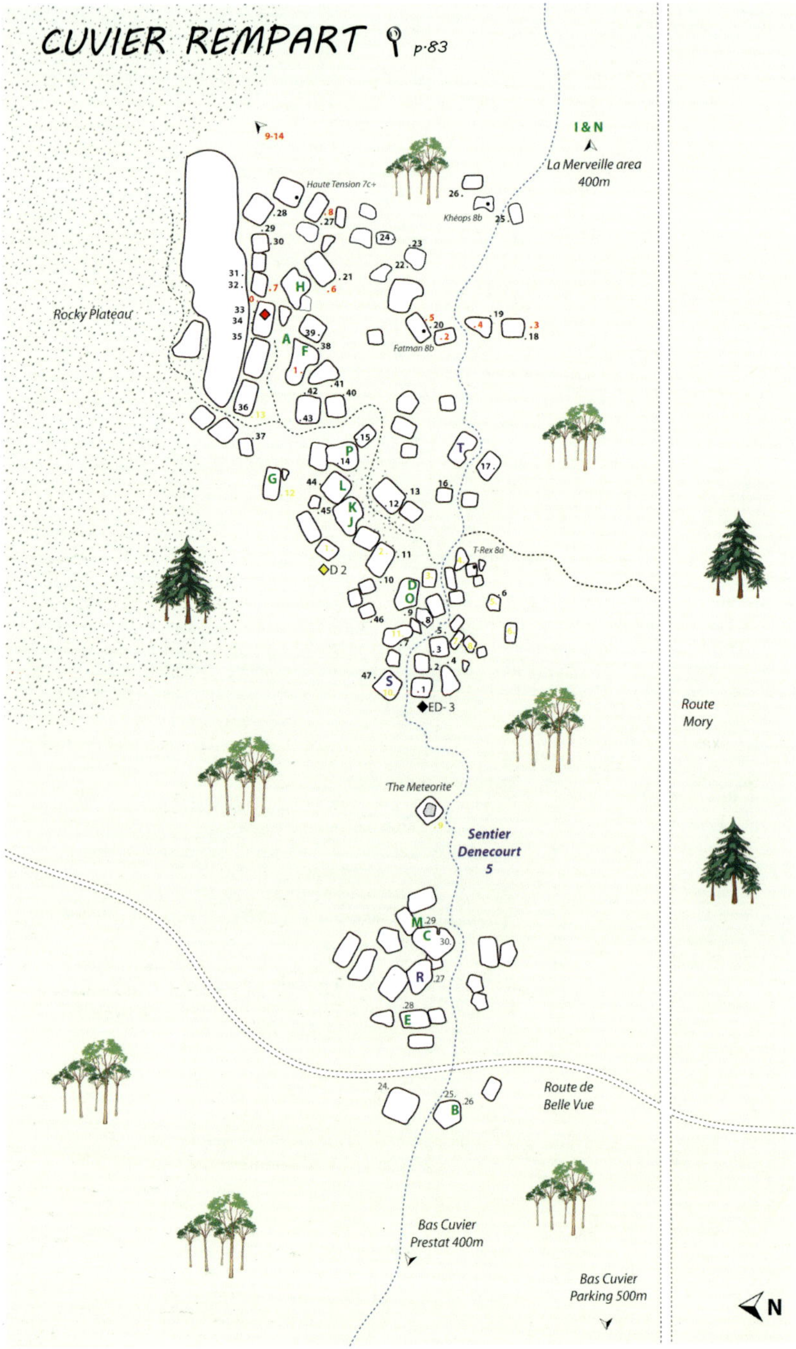
CUVIER REMPART
p.83
I & N
La Merveille area
400m
Haute Tension 7c+
Khéops 8b
Rocky Plateau
Fatman 8b
T-Rex 8a
D 2
ED- 3
'The Meteorite'
Sentier
Denecourt
5
Route
Mory
Route de
Belle Vue
Bas Cuvier
Prestat 400m
Bas Cuvier
Parking 500m
N

CUVIER REMPART

BLOC NOTES >>> 'Rempart' is a quiet area but home to some of the forest's hardest and most famous problems, including the 'big three' 7c's: *Big Boss*, *Tristesse* and *Fourmis Rouges*. These are all impressive high lines for the aspirant Bleausard. The area saw the first circuit in 1947 (Red AD-) as an alpine training idea. The rock is beautiful, often slopey and well textured, so perfect for hard problems. As it lies on a rocky ridge, it is exposed and dries quickly. This was also where Pierre Allain climbed the first 5+ *L'Angle Allain* (try it in modern boots, it's still hard to stick). This is not a beginner's area and the older circuits are a little faded and overgrown. It is a superb venue if you are climbing 6c and above, as there are many absorbing test pieces. If you feel like solitude and spending your time on just one problem alone, this is probably the place to go.

ACCESS >>> From the Cuvier car-park walk east. There are two approaches: 1. Via the blue-marked *Sentier Denecourt 5*, which winds throught the forest, walking straight past classic test boulders such as *La Prestat*, *Duroxmanie*, *Big Boss*, *Fatman* etc. From *Duroxmanie*, continue along the blue path past the perched stone feature of *L'Aérolithe* ('The Meteorite') to the jumble of boulders under the high ridge, which is the Rempart area. Look out for 'lettered' boulders R, S and T as useful landmarks on the blue path (see map). 2. The *Route Mory de Neuflieux* is a more direct path to reach the side-paths up to Cuvier East and Cuvier Rempart (as well as the giant bloc of *La Merveille*, 1km east at the next junction of paths). The blue path can be gained from the main path at the crossroads of the *Route de Belle Vue* and the *Route Mory*.

CIRCUITS >>> The first circuit in the forest was the ◆ red circuit (AD- no. 1), it has 16 problems from 2 to 3+. and starts on the south face of the ridge on the way up to the 'Rempart'. The ◇ yellow circuit (D no. 2) has 13 problems and there are two black circuits: the ◆ 'Trivellini' circuit (TD- no. 2) which is a stretched circuit of 30 problems heading east from Bas Cuvier to Cuvier Rempart (from the junction with the Route de Belle Vue, the circuit ends from problems 24 to the last number 30, in the 'Duroxmanie' sector). Then there is the ◆ Rempart black circuit (ED- no. 3), starting 40m after the 'Meteorite', from where it meanders up to the Rempart plateau. There are 47 problems , some of them highball.

TEST PIECES >>>

❐ A. *L'Angle Allain*	5+	Right hand wall via sharp arête on smears. Left side 6a.
❐ B. *La Mummery*	6b	Black 26. Smooth round rib and groove.
❐ C. *Duroxmanie*	6c	Black 29. Classic shield of rock finishing right via hidden pocket.
❐ D. *Septième Ciel*	6c	Right to left lip right of *C'Était Demain*.
❐ E. *Festin Pierre*	7a	Black 28 var. Slopey ledge to twin crimps to top. Heel-hook.
❐ F. *Laser*	7a	Flat slab and nicks in corridor down from *L'Angle Allain*.
❐ G. *Immodium*	7a	Dyno the bulge right of yellow 12 to high right sloper. SS 7b.
❐ H. *Noir Désir*	7b	Undercling roof via slopey pods leftwards. Direct is 7c.
❐ I. *Bleau's Art*	7b	Scooped overhanging prow 40m left of *La Merveille* above *Route Mory*.
❐ J. *Big Boss*	7c	The overhanging flake and lip above sandpit, trend left at top.
❐ K. *Fourmis Rouges*	7c	The crack just right of *Big Boss* to slopey top-out.
❐ L. *Tristesse*	7c	High blunt arête on the next bloc up above sandy landing.
❐ M. *Michel Ange*	7c	Hard gaston/undercling problem just right of *Duroxmanie*.
❐ N. *La Merveille*	8a	Obvious blunt and highball arête on back of giant bloc marked 'B'.
❐ O. *C'Était Demain*	8a	Stone start the high wall via slopey holds just up from path.
❐ P. *Big Golden*	8a	SS the rounded boss bloc to lip, trend left to mantle. Stand up 7c+.

❐ Merveille bloc

❐ Laser

❒ Rempart > C'Était Demain

❒ Rempart > Big Boss

❒ Rempart > Big Golden 8a

❒ Rempart > Tristesse

❒ Cuvier > Aerodynamite

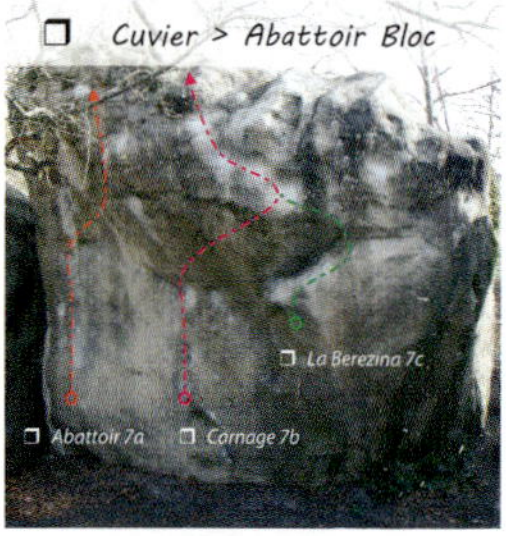

❒ Cuvier > Abattoir Bloc

❒ Cuvier > La Marie Rose

❒ Cuvier > Hypothèse

❒ Cuvier > Charcuterie

❒ Cuvier > Biceps Mou Bloc

❒ Rocher Canon > Compressman 7a > Photo © Dan Varian

❒ Rocher Canon > Orca

❒ Rocher Canon > Chasseur de Prises

❒ Rocher Canon > Délivrance

❒ Rocher Canon > Levitation

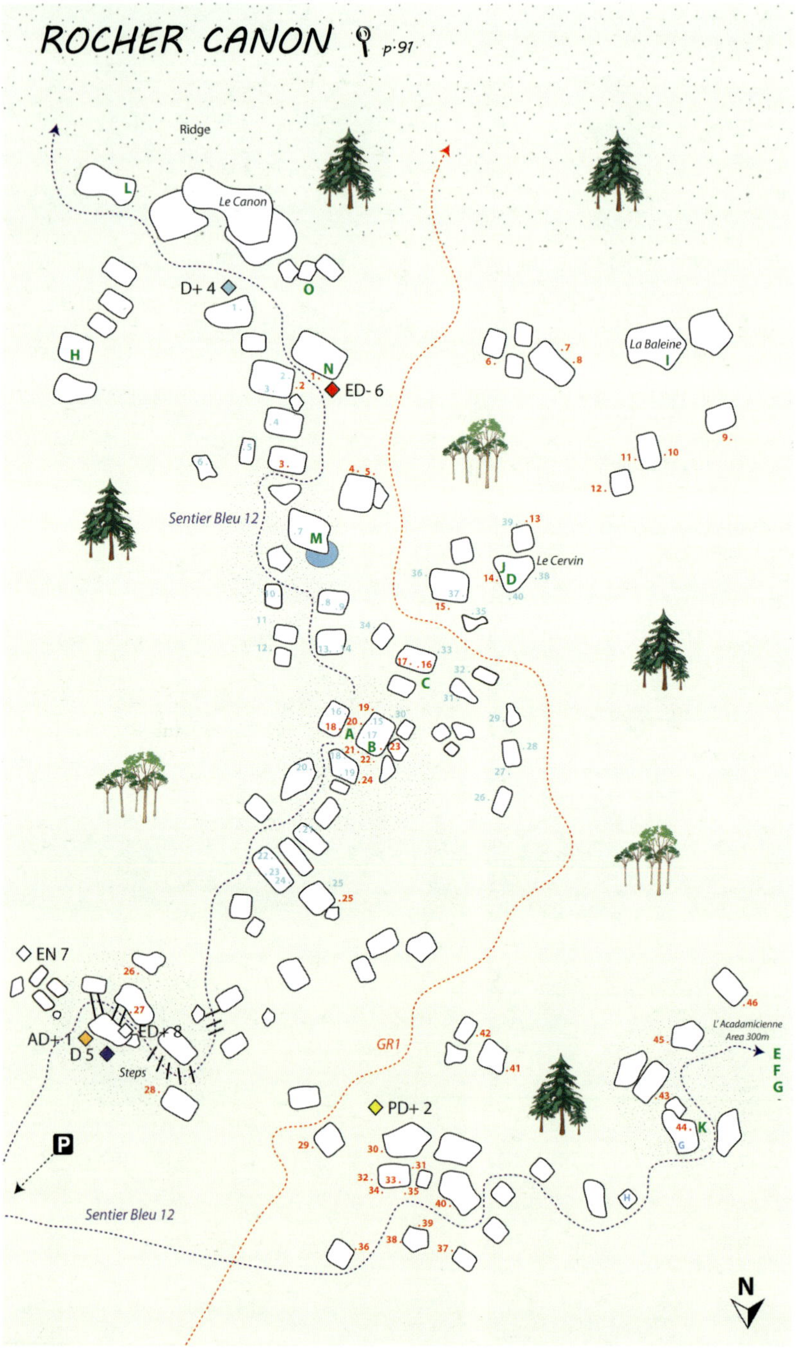
ROCHER CANON
p.91
Ridge
Le Canon
L
O
D+ 4
H
N
ED- 6
La Baleine
I
Sentier Bleu 12
M
Le Cervin
J
D
C
A
B
EN 7
AD+ 1
ED+ 8
D 5
Steps
GR1
PD+ 2
L'Acadamicienne
Area 300m
E
F
G
K
P
Sentier Bleu 12
N

ROCHER CANON

BLOC NOTES >>> Rocher Canon is often overlooked, due to the proximity of Cuvier. However, it has a secluded feel and reasonably good landings. There are some unique test pieces such as *Chasseur de Prises* and a great ambience amongst the pines. The *Sentier Bleu* path skirts most of the bouldering.

ACCESS >>> Accessible on foot from nearby Bois-le-Rois train station (take the GR1 via *La Route de la Perlure* and La *Route du Lancer* for 20 minutes). If driving, take the road north signed to Melun from the *Carrefour de la Croix* (big cross and traffic lights) on the N7 between Fontainebleau and Barbizon. Drive about 4km north and as the road swings right after a descent, watch out for a left turn onto the *Route du Lancer* (easy to miss) which swings left to the parking area. The main boulders are a short walk up through the steps.

CIRCUITS >>> The ◇ white kids' circuit (EN no. 7) starts by the path on the way to the blocs, 50m from the parking. The ◆ yellow circuit (PD+ no. 2) has 48 easy problems up to 3+ and starts on the north face of the 'Canon' boulder on the ridge. The ◆ orange circuit (AD+ no. 1) has 43 problems and starts on a boulder to the left on path up the steps. The ◆ dark blue circuit (D no. 5) has 41 problems and starts on a boulder on the right after the top of the steps. The ◆ sky blue circuit (D+ no. 4) has 40 problems and starts on the boulder opposite the giant 'Canon' boulder on ridge. The ◆ red circuit (ED- no. 6) has 46 excellent problems, starting on a boulder just down from the the 'Canon' boulder by the blue path. The harder ◇ white circuit (ED+ no. 8) has 24 problems, the best of which are 1, 4, 8, 10, 16, 17, 20, 21.

TEST PIECES >>>

❒ A. *Le Cheval d'Arcon*	5+	Light blue 17. Layback the fine arête just left of *Styrax*.
❒ B. *Styrax*	6a+	Red 22 is a classic wall above a sandy pit, toe positions essential.
❒ C. *Le Bossu*	6b+	Red 16, undercling up to blunt arête, requires good body positioning.
❒ D. *Superlative*	6b+	Slab using high arête on *Le Cervin* ('Matterhorn') bloc.
❒ E. *L'Académicienne*	6c+	R-L low traverse on long bloc just below blue path 'F' bloc.
❒ F. *Rêve de Pierre*	7a	Roofed arête on 'F' bloc on blue path 300m west of main area.
❒ G. *Monsieur Plus*	7a	SS blue-marked overhang and crack above path to 'F' bloc.
❒ H. *Chasseur de Prises*	7a	White 24, the lipped wall has a hard sloping finish, 40m left of red 1.
❒ I. *Orca*	7a	Right hand bulge of roof marked *La Baleine* (LH SS 7c+).
❒ J. *Délivrance*	7a+	Slab direct left of *Superlative*, on *Le Cervin* ('Matterhorn') bloc.
❒ K. *La Lévitation*	7a+	L-R low traverse of pocketed roof to exit right crack.
❒ L. *La Théorie du Chaos*	7b	White 23, on bloc behind cave on ridge, a slopey prow. SS 7b+.
❒ M. *La Mare Droite*	7b	Bloc above wet pit, travel right from pocket right of tree exit.
❒ N. *Le Chaînon Manquant*	7b	Right of red 1, climb wall using heel on arête, exit left of tree.
❒ O. *Full Metal Jacket*	7b+	Small wedged bloc. SS 7c+. Arête bloc to left is *Compressman* 7a.

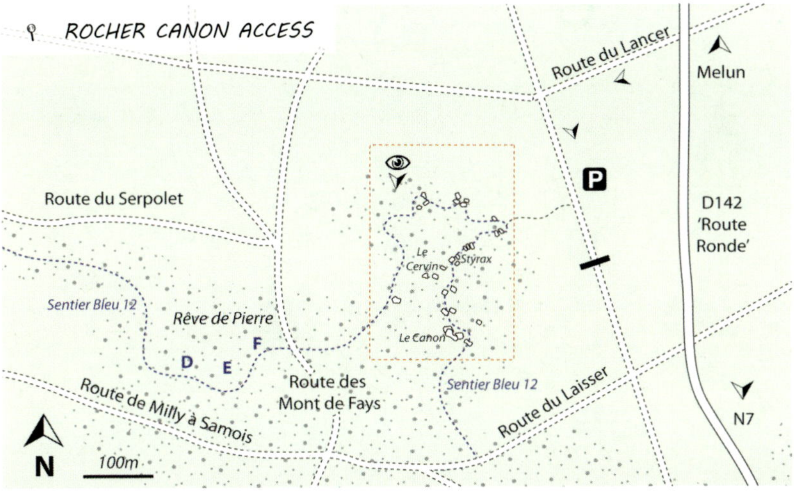

ÉLÉPHANT

p.93

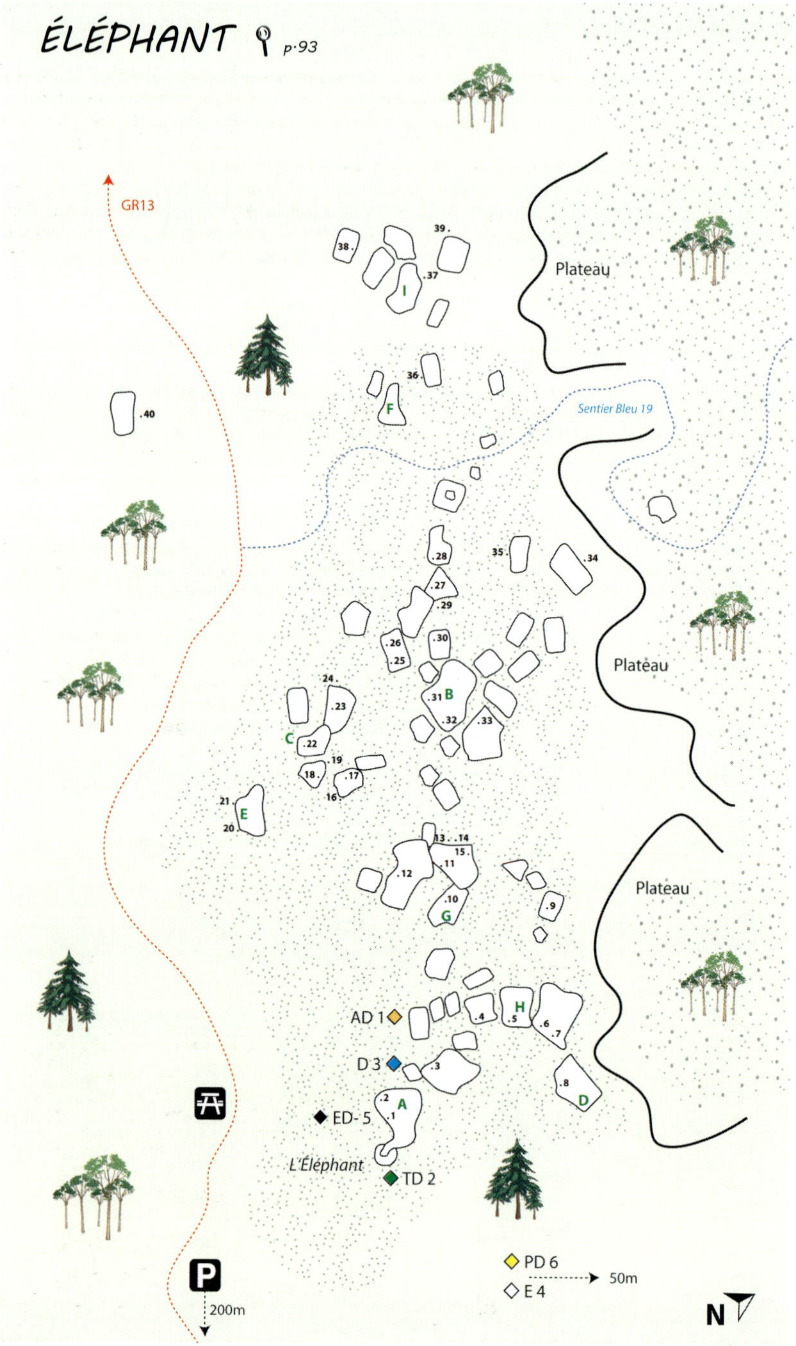

ÉLÉPHANT

BLOC NOTES >>> This is one of the most picturesque bouldering venues in south Fontainebleau, due to the numerous bizarre natural sculptures such as the famous *Elephant* boulder. This is a sandy area and the rock is soft, so please do not climb here after rain as holds can snap and feet can cause erosion. It is best in cool, sunny, breezy weather when it is very popular. There are quieter areas such as Elephant West & North, and Mont Simonet, as well as the giant massif of Dame Jouanne a little further north.

ACCESS >>> The massif lies 1km north of the village of L'Archant on the small road leading to Dame Jouanne. If coming from the D16 road from La Chapelle la Reine, take a left at the small roundabout at L' Archant and swing round the north of the village to a signposted road left leading north to Dame Jouanne. For *Elephant* park on the left or right at the first forest clearing by an old water pump – *The Elephant* lies in the sandy bay just out of sight west over a rise and opposite picnic tables.

CIRCUITS >>> One ◇ kids' circuit starts at the steps up to the plateau to the east of the parking and heads west around *The Elephant*. The ◇ yellow circuit (PD no. 6) has 49 easy problems and starts near the road in the eastern area and meanders up onto the plateau rocks. The ◇ orange circuit (AD no. 1) has 44 problems and 3 variants, starting just north of *The Elephant*. The long ◆ blue circuit (D no. 3) has 84 problems plus many variants and heads clockwise round the plateau from *The Elephant*. The ◆ green circuit (TD no. 2) has 31 problems and starts at *The Elephant* and meanders round the west of the plateau. The excellent black circuit starts at *The Elephant* and heads north-west to finish at the distinctive holed wall of *La Dalle à Polly*.

TEST PIECES >>>

❒ A. *L'Éléphant*	6a	Black 1 is a classic problem via sidepulls and pockets, with toe-work essential.
❒ B. *Le Toit du Loup*	6b	The flying pocketed roof of black 31 is another bold classic.
❒ C. *La Voie Michaud*	6c	The groove of black 22 is a clever exercise in technique.
❒ D. *Le Pilier Droyer*	6c+	The eared arête wall right of Black 8 is balancy, reach left at top.
❒ E. *Le Lépreux*	7a	Undercut up left between black 20 and 21, gain slopers then dyno!
❒ F. *Le Coeur*	7a	Gain the 'heart' crimps and reach high to the hanging crack, morpho.
❒ G. *La Barre Fixe*	7b	Sit start up leaning wall of pockets direct. Dyno to top from big pocket.
❒ H. *Coup de Lune*	7b+	Left of Black 5, power up the overhanging flange to edges.
❒ I. *Envie d' Ailes*	7c	Bloc 50m left of *Le Coeur*. Fingery wall from the ledge, left then right.

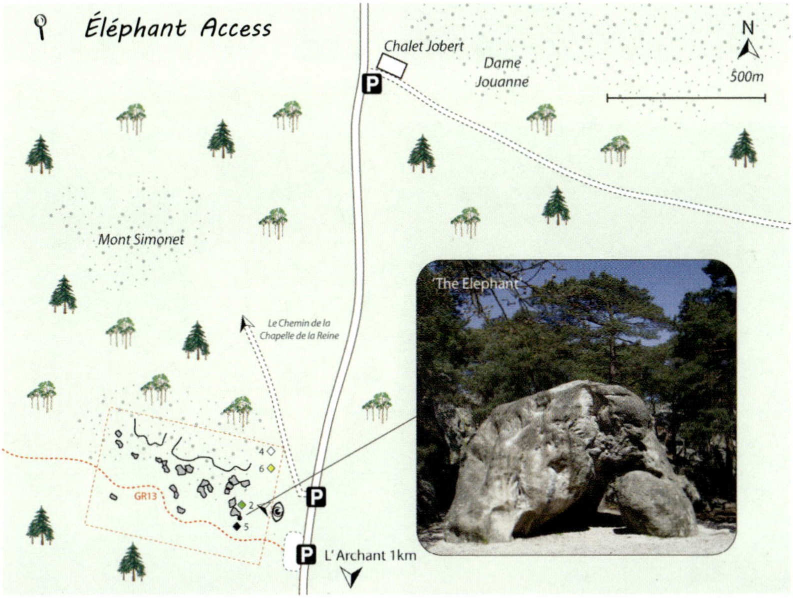

❒ Éléphant > Le Bouton 7a > Black 26

❒ Le Coeur > Photo © Arran Curran

❒ Le Lepreux

❒ La Barre Fixe

❒ La Voie Michaud > Photo © Roddy MacKenzie

❒ Éléphant > Le Coeur landscape

❒ Éléphant > Blue Circuit highballing

❒ Vicky Mayes on Figure de Proue

❒ Black 5 Photo © Stuart Stronach

❒ The Blue Circuit

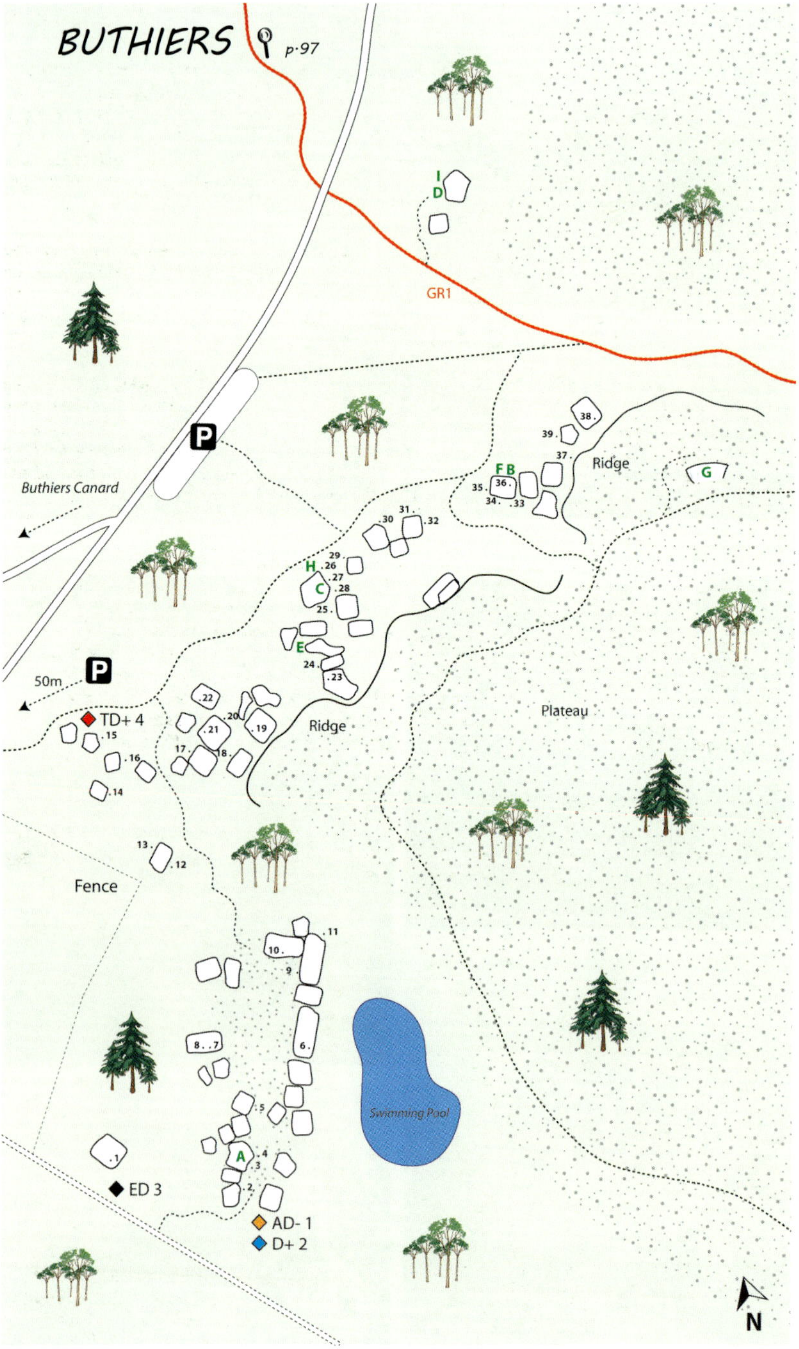
BUTHIERS
p.97
GR1
Buthiers Canard
50m
TD+ 4
ED 3
AD- 1
D+ 2
Ridge
Ridge
Plateau
Fence
Swimming Pool
N
A
B
C
D
E
F
G
H
I
1
2
3
4
5
6
7
8
9
10
11
12
13
14
15
16
17
18
19
20
21
22
23
24
25
26
27
28
29
30
31
32
33
34
35
36
37
38
39

BUTHIERS

BLOC NOTES >>> Buthiers is an open air playground for all. Tennis grounds, boulder fields, swimming pools and even assault courses surround a large public parking area south of Malesherbes, consequently it can feel busy in summer. There are three main bouldering areas, the first on the roadside at the Auberge 'Canard', the next known as 'Tennis' and the quieter *Massif de L' Il*, which has north and south aspects along the low ridge overlooking the 'Piscine' (swimming pool). This is probably the best area with some singular test pieces and a very famous and enjoyable black circuit, created by the *Bleausard* Alain Michaud in the 1970s. Care must be taken with often highball problems.

ACCESS >>> At the crossroads and traffic lights entering Malesherbes from the east, take a left turn signposted to Buthiers. The road passes the Auberge Canard and arrives at the large parking area where boulders on the left stand by the tennis courts. Continue along the one-way system to the south side and continue northeast 500m to a long parking space by the woods and the *Massif de L'Il* on the right. From here, most of the classics can be accessed in five minutes at most.

CIRCUITS >>> The ◇ yellow circuit (F no. 5) has 23 easy problems and starts 200m to the southwest of the main area. The ◆ orange circuit (AD- no. 1) has 44 problems starting beside the blue circuit at the south of the ridge near the swimming pool. The ◆ blue circuit (D+ no. 2) has 42 problems starting beside the orange circuit at the south of the ridge, also near the swimming pool. The ◆ red circuit (TD+ no. 4) has 35 problems starting by the parking path in the west of the area. The ◆ black circuit (ED no. 3) has 39 problems and one variant, starting on a bloc to the south-east of the ridge, just along the main track to the pool.

TEST PIECES >>>

❒ A. *Le Surplomb du Marbre*	6a	Black 3 is a classic marbled bulge with technical crimping.
❒ B. *Swing Medium*	6b	Black 36 is a tough undercut test piece to turn the blunt arête.
❒ C. *La Super Fresque*	6c	The crimpy wall of black 27, left of *La Fresque* groove (5+).
❒ D. *Attention Chef d' Oeuvre*	7a	The classic high wall through slots to trend left at top.
❒ E. *Lady Big Claque/le Flipper*	7a+	Highball bear-hugging prow to top slopers, trend right at top.
❒ F. *Strappal*	7b+	Right of black 36, crossover crimps to undercut to top.
❒ G. *Magic Bus*	7b+	Power out of the depths of the low hidden cave, left or right . . .
❒ H. *Appartenance*	7c	The steep right side of the arête beside *La Fresque* groove.
❒ I. *Partage*	8a+	The high leaning arête left of *Attention Chef d' Oeuvre*.

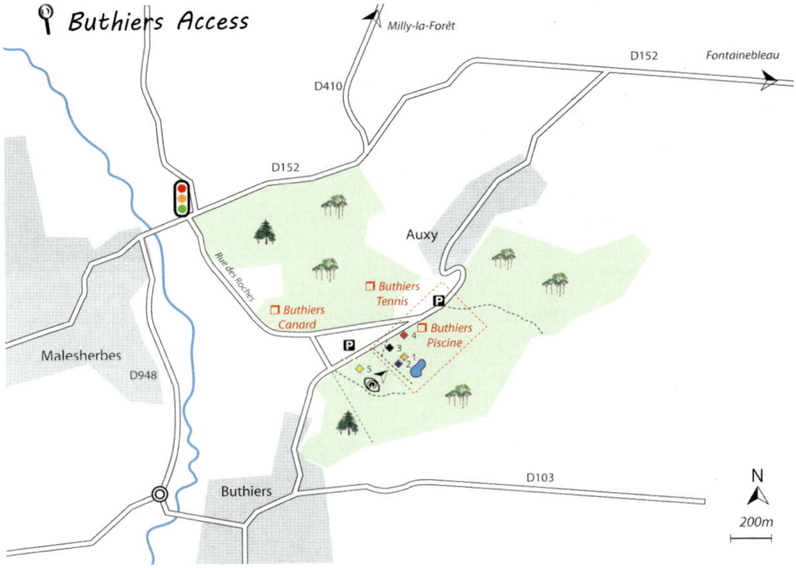

❐ Swing Medium

❐ Black 19 > La Duchesse

❐ Strappal 7b+

❐ Backwoods Buthiers

❒ Buthiers > Magic Bus

❒ Partage 8a & Chef d 'Oeuvre 7a

❒ Black 3 > Surplomb du Marbre

❒ La Yano > Black 18

❒ The Black Circuit at Buthiers

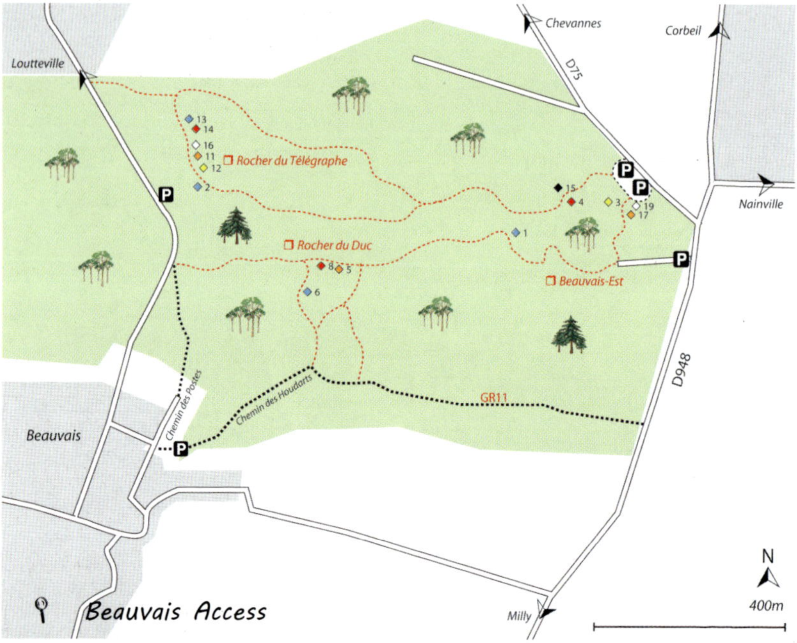

❒ Beauvais > Étrave à Sucre

❒ St Germain > Megalithe

❒ St Germain > Delire Onrique

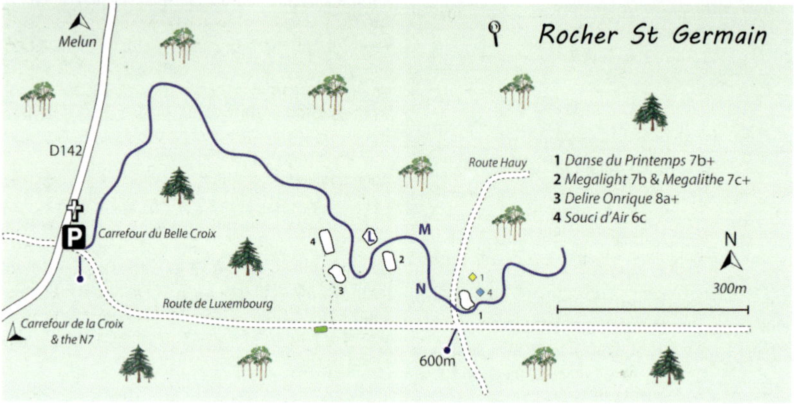

FONTAINEBLEAU NORTH

Fomtainebleau is a vast forest and hidden in the dips, hollows and plateaux of the forest are less frequented areas with quality individual blocs and some old circuits, many of which are coming back into fashion. If you do wish a little solitude and just want to get that 'backwoods' feel, or you want to scope out new problems, it is worth taking along your IGN map of the forest and go hunting! You may find yourself staying in the south, in which case you may want to visit *Petit Bois*, *Mammouths* or *Dame Jouanne*, or if you are in the north of the forest the vast expanse of *Coquibus* is an adventure, or the more popular *Beauvais* plateau is fun. Oddly, close to Fontainebleau town itself there are many venues with a 'lost' feel about them, within walking distance of the train station: *Rocher St Germain/Cassepot*, *Mont Aigu*, *Calvaire*, *Bouligny* or *Rocher d' Avon*. Here is a selection of some of the backwoods venues you may wish to explore further.

Beauvais

North-west of the Trois Pignons, this is a pleasant and popular area on a wooded ridge above the town of Beauvais. The east-west ridge provides low boulders and a sunny atmosphere amongst the trees. There are several areas, including a number of circuits at *Rocher du Duc* just north of the village, but the best area is probably the ridge boulders on the north-east side of the forested hill of Beauvais. The test piece to seek out is the superb 7b+ pillar of ❐ *Étrave à Sucre* right of black/white 4. From Milly, take the D948 north through Moigny-sur-École. For the popular *Beauvais Est* area, continue 5km over two crossroads to an easily missed left turn signposted to Chevannes (D75). After 250m there is parking on the left. To access the main ridge, head straight uphill. The main ridge has good circuits:

◇ Kids' white circuit (E- no. 19) Starts just south of the east side of the parking. 45 problems.
◆ Yellow (PD+ no. 3) is an uphill clockwise circuit of 46 problems.
◆ Orange (AD+ no. 17) is an uphill clockwise circuit of 46 problems.
◇ Kids' white circuit (E+ no. 10) starts just south of the west side of the parking. 42 problems.
◆ Pale yellow (F no. 10) is a circuit of 40 problems starting just south of the west side of the parking.
◆ Blue (D no. 1) is a circuit of 50 problems and 9 variants starting 150m uphill from the west side of the parking.
◆ Red (TD+ no. 4) is a circuit of 40 problems starting off the west side of the parking 100m uphill.
◆ Black (ED+ no. 15) is a circuit heading uphill 100m southwest from the west side of the parking. 30 problems and 8 variants, 6a to 7c.

Rocher du Duc and *Rocher du Télégraphe* lie further west on the ridge and are more easily accessible from the town of Beauvais. The circuits at *Rocher du Duc* can be accessed along the *Chemin des Houdarts* and north uphill. Park in the woods off the *Chemin des Postes*. The parking for *Rocher du Télégraphe* lies on the Loutteville road, on the right just after the bend.

Rocher St Germain/Cassepot

Excellent and quiet test piece areas east of the Cuvier massif north of the old roadway that is the *Route de Luxembourg* and just north of the massive Hippodrome racecourse. The boulders lie on the winding *Sentier Bleu* 4-3 path, whose alphabet-feature rocks are a good reference point for finding the specific boulders and hard problems such as the *Mégalithe*. There are lots of boulders and hidden gems in this area. Follow the blue way-marked rocks and trees if you get lost. The west-east ridge continues across the D606 to an area known as *Cassepot* (Roches Grises, Oranges & Roses).

From the *Carrefour de la Libération* roundabout (the crazy main roundabout at Fontainebleau) go north on the main N7 as for Cuvier, but at the next roundabout *Carrefour de la Croix* (with the cross) turn right towards Melun. As the road rises up a hill there is parking on the right by a white cross (*Belle Croix*). Turn east downhill along the *Route de Luxembourg* path and after a few hundred metres on a flatter sand section, there is a blunt stone with a green mark. A few yards after this is a rough path on the left leading 50m up to the *Sentier Bleu* path with the boulders, with the impressive high overhanging mantle of ❐ *Délire Onrique* 8a+. The bloc of *Mégalithe* lies further along the path to the right from this. The large bloc to the north of *Délire Onrique* has a good dyno problem in ❐ *Soucis d'Air* 6c, which is 8a from the sit start ledge.

Another option is to walk further east to turn left onto the *Route Huay* to where the *Sentier Bleu* path crosses over. On the left is the start of the ◆ blue circuit and the main area. On the right is the esoteric ❐ *Danse de Printemps* boulder – a right to left traverse on slopers in the narrow corridor (a superb Font 7b+). Return via the Sentier Bleu for the main boulders.

For *Mégalithe*, continue from *Danse* west across the path to the Sentier Bleu path and pass the N and M blocs to the L boulder. ❐ *Mégalithe* 7c+ is just before and downhill of this and is the obvious north overhanging wall. ❐ *Mégalight* 7b takes the south arête, mantle right over the flat stone. The wall to the right is ❐ *Mégalutte* 6b+ and the flake and roof between this and *Mégalithe* is ❐ *Mégalatte* 7a. All could be described as 'mega'!

❒ Bouligny > Amok 8a > Photo © Dan Varian

❒ Mont Ussy > Ussy Cat

❒ Mont Ussy > Roche Hercule

❒ Gorges du Houx > Gargantoit

❒ Gorges du Houx > L'Inaccessible Absolu

❒ Calvaire > L' Aplat du Gain 8a > Dan Varian

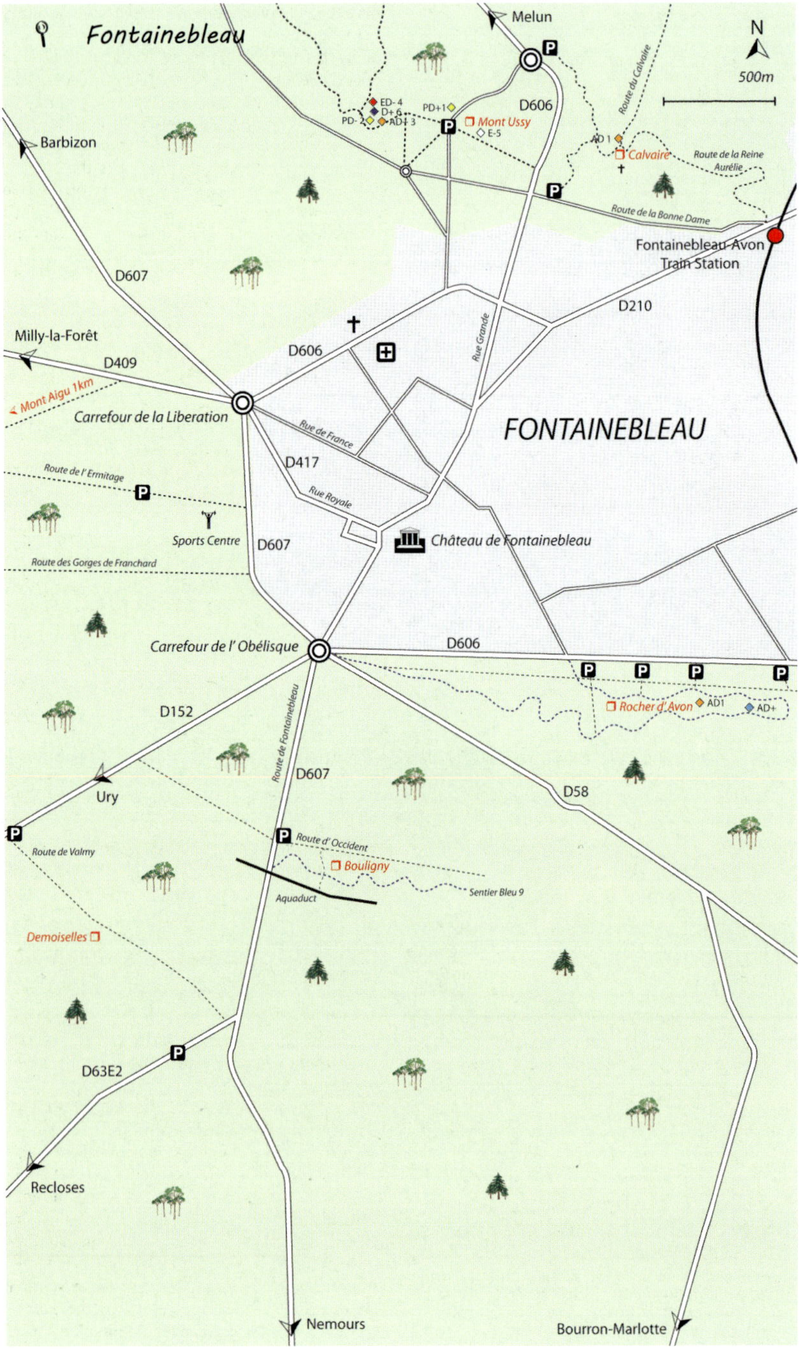
Fontainebleau
N
500m
Melun
D606
ED- 4
D+ 6
PD- 2
AD+ 3
PD+1
Mont Ussy
E-5
Route du Calvaire
AD 1
Calvaire
Route de la Reine Aurélie
Barbizon
Route de la Bonne Dame
Fontainebleau-Avon Train Station
D607
D210
Milly-la-Forêt
D606
D409
Rue Grande
Mont Aigu 1km
Carrefour de la Liberation
FONTAINEBLEAU
Rue de France
D417
Route de l' Ermitage
Rue Royale
Sports Centre
D607
Château de Fontainebleau
Route des Gorges de Franchard
Carrefour de l' Obélisque
D606
D152
Rocher d' Avon
AD1
AD+
Route de Fontainebleau
D607
Ury
D58
Route d' Occident
Route de Valmy
Bouligny
Aquaduct
Sentier Bleu 9
Demoiselles
D63E2
Recloses
Nemours
Bourron-Marlotte

FONTAINEBLEAU TOWN

There are several areas within 1 hour's walking distance of Fontainebleau town, most notably the *Calvaire* sector on the ridge north of the town, and the *Mont Ussy* boulders. Outlying areas can be accessed by car, bike or a walk from the train station.

Calvaire

This massive roof can easily be walked to from the Font Avon train station along the *Sentier Bleu 2* (behind Hotel de Gare), or along the *Route de la Reine Aurélie*. Follow the ridge trending west past the *Croix de Calvaire*. There is one ◆ orange circuit. On the left of the roof is the famous three move 8a ❐ *L'Aplat du Gain*. Recent erosion has made the main roof very unsafe, so do not climb on it.

Mont Ussy

This is a quiet area with red and white marked problems. From the big roundabout *Carrefour de la Libération* follow signs for the hospital and Avon (D606), go past the cemetery and turn left. Continue into the forest and park at the *Route du Mont Ussy* car-park. The obvious *Roche Hercule* is just on the right along the *Sentier Bleu 1*. The pocketed prow is a super 6c ❐ *Le Pilier de la Roche Hercule*, while the white-arrowed wall to the left is the excellent 7a ❐ *Gazoline*. For more test pieces, follow the path west into the forest for half a kilometre and find the steep problems on the right in the cave *La Grotte des Montussiennes*, such as ❐ *Ussy Cat* 7a+ (red 11 bis, climb the crack but exit to the right dynamically). Finishing left is red 11 ❐ *Ussy Tôt Fait* 6b+. The front prow over the fence is the hard and dynamic ❐ *L'Être Hâve* 7c.

Mont Aigu

This hill venue is accessed from *La Faisanderie* parking on the *Route de l' Ermitage*, west of the Sports Centre on the D607. To reach the boulders, follow the *Route du Levraut* for about 1km, heading southwest, then turn right onto the *Route des Gorges de Franchard* and you'll find the ◆ blue circuit on the right after about 400m, along the Sentier Bleu. ❐ *Montée Divine* is the excellent 7a split arête left of blue 7 shortly up the path on the left.

Gorges du Houx

This venue is a little stretched but has some classic problems. It lies on a low ridge north of the *Routes des Gorges de Franchard* between Mont Aigu and the large Franchard parking at *L'Ermitage* on the Route Ronde, which is the best approach if you have a car. Park at the Hermitage car-park and head east across the road to follow the *Routes des Gorges de Franchard*. Follow this downhill for 1km to a left turn onto the *Route du Renard*, go north for 300m and when you find the blue path, turn right to the main area. The blue way-marked path (Sentier Bleu 8) leads through various feature blocs to a cave system boulder marked 'H'. ❐ *Gargantoit* 7a+ takes the striking leaning arête in the bivouac. Further west on the blue path is the almighty prow (marked 'F') of ❐ *L'Inaccessible Absolu*, a highball 7c just off the *Carrefour de Franchière*. Most walk on by!

Rochers des Demoiselles

Gain the *Route de Valmy* parking on the D152 , follow *La Route de Valmy* east for 900m, the ◆ orange circuit (AD no. 1) is on the right after the crossing with *La Route du Champ de Manoeuvre*. The blocs lie along the *Sentier Bleu 9* uphill to the south. ❐ *L'Olive* is the crack test piece (7a direct), found opposite the *Sentier Bleu* 'I' boulder (on the bloc with 26 Orange). Retrace the blue path back east (reversing the alphabet!) along the ridge to find numerous other test pieces. ❐ *Hybris* is a 7b+ lipped overhang just to the west of the *Route de la Séduction* (just south of the junction with the *Route de Valmy* near the car park).

Rocher d' Avon

Go south from the *Carrefour de la Libération* and at the next roundabout (*Obélisque*) take the busy D606 Montereau exit east. After a road on the left park at the third lay-by on the right at the *Route de la Percée*. Go south across the *Carrefour de Mayenne* and shortly after join the *Sentier Bleu 10* east (left) to find the boulders. The obvious feature bloc of *La Dame Jeanne d'Avon* has an excellent high west wall called ❐ *Fil à Plomb* at Font 7b+. The ◆ orange circuit starts just before this.

Rocher de Bouligny

A good strung-out collection of blocs and virtual circuits with some fine test pieces. To access drive south on the D607 from the *Carrefour de l' Obélisque* and turn back on yourself at the next junction to park on the east side of the road at the *Route d' Occident* car-park, 150m to the north of the aqueduct. Two main sectors lie on both sides of *La Route Pompadour* (the first path on the right). Most test pieces lie on blocs on the ridge along the blue path. ❐ *Damoclès* 7a is a slopey traverse on the low roof of the blue-starred bloc on the blue path 100m east of the *Route Pompadour*. ❐ *Amok* 8a is a superb slopey wall in a pit, near the underground part of the aqueduct, 50m south of the blue-starred boulders on the blue path (*Damoclès*). ❐ *Les Beaux Quartiers* 8a sit starts an overhanging pillar south (uphill) of the *Route d' Occident* about 150m along (6c stand-up).

Dame Jouanne > Angle Parfait

Petit Bois > Big Jim

Petit Bois > La Baleine

Mammouths > Osiris

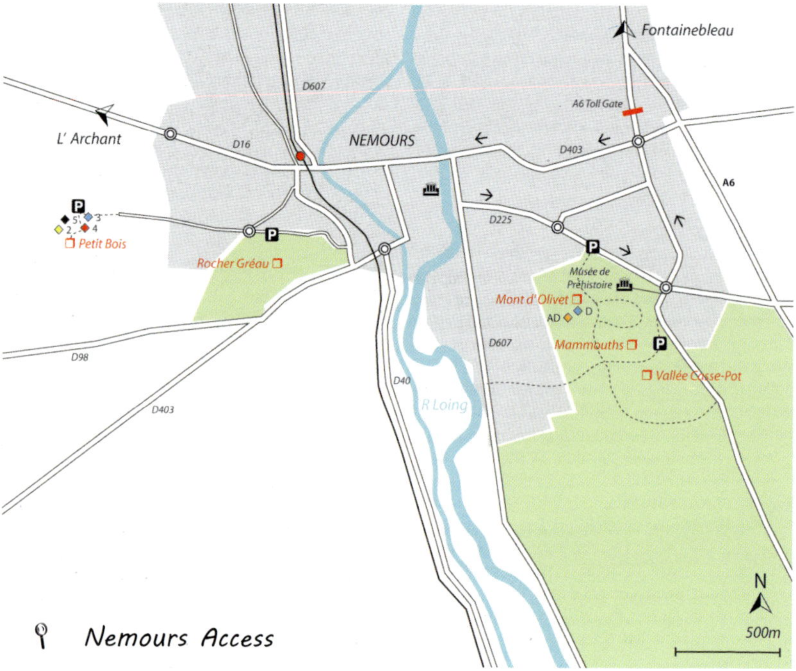

Nemours Access

L' ARCHANT

The southern area has a few quiet areas with exciting test pieces outwith the main areas of Éléphant and Buthiers. They lie west of the town of Nemours and south of the D16 road to L'Archant, from which they can be approached. They are a good alternative if you find Éléphant too busy! *Petit Bois, Puiselet* and *Rocher Gréau* are the best areas, though *Les Mammouths* east of Nemours has excellent blocs worth a singular visit.

Dame Jouanne

This giant massif is generally highball with some bad landings, but it is worth a visit for one or two classics and the ◇ white/black circuit, or if you want to do some roped climbing! The ridge has two giant boulders or pinnacles, the left one is *La Dame Jouanne* and the right one is *La Caroline*, which are useful as reference markers. Further east lies the massif of Maunory which has a good ◆ red circuit. Both areas are easily accessed from the large car-park by the Chalet Jobert. Dame Jouanne is signposted from L'Archant village and passes the Éléphant area before the Chalet Jobert appears on the right 1km later, park at the end of the large car park. The boulders are obvious under the ridge, which can be ascended on paths to the viewpoint plateau.

To get to the classic ❐ *Angle Parfait* 7b (a wonderful and technical arête), veer uphill left past *La Dame Jouanne* pillar crag and gain the flat plateau, head right along the viewpoint top until a small deep-cut narrow corridor leads down towards a conservation area at the top of the boulder cluster above *La Caroline*. The obvious edge is climbed via tenuous laybacks on its left side.

Maunory

For the Maunory area, take the *Chemin de la Chapelle-la-Reine à Nemours* from the car-park east until you can veer off left on the *Sentier Bleu 19* which swings right underneath the boulders and leads to steps. A little before the steps to the left of the area there is a good 7b dyno called ❐ *Movement Activated* on the scooped pillar right of Red 11. If you like jumps, also try the excellent 7b problem ❐ *Morphomaniacs* on the hanging bulge left of Blue 34 (straight uphill through the large boulders). There are 3 circuits: ◆ orange (AD- no. 1) which has 54 problems and 6 variants. The ◆ blue circuit (D no. 2) has 71 problems and 3 variants. The ◆ red circuit (TD+ no. 3) has 36 problems and starts to the south of the *Sentier Bleu 13* path about 400m along the main path (east from parking), then crosses the Blue path heading west and then north uphill to the plateau.

NEMOURS

Rocher Gréau

If driving along the D16 from L'Archant, continue into Nemours and take the right turn (Av. Leopold Pelletier) just before the railway crossing. Go south for 600m on the D98 , turn right and drive along to parking at the Hotel de Ville. The boulders lie in the park opposite. This area is one for the highest-level climbers, if you feel like one, have a go at the immediately steep Grand Toit boulder, with ❐ *Chaos* 8b taking the obvious horizontal crack and roof.

Petit Bois

'Little Wood' is a recently developed area with newish circuits and some great test pieces. The approach is the same for Rocher Gréau, but continue west along the *Chemin de la Messe* over the roundabout straight on into the forest along a track by a field. The boulders lie on the hill above the car-park, veer right for the classic problem of ❐ *La Baleine*, an obvious round-lipped 7a+ roof that looks something like a whale! It lies left of the start of the red and black circuits and is Black no. 7. Also worth doing is the incredible high pocketed wall of ❐ *Big Jim* 6c, just downhill of *La Baleine*. The wall gets harder the higher you climb and the crux throw at the top for jugs is where most people jump off.

Puiselet

Also known as 'Paradis' - this area lies just west of the town of Puiselet south of the D16 between L'Archant and Nemours. After a sharp bend in Puiselet village turn right on the steep hill and follow this to another right turn onto the Rue Grande, at the end of which turn left onto the *Impasse des Plantes* track which leads to discreet parking near a sandpit. Walk past a line of trees to turn right across fields to a lone tree, from where a path leads into the forest and a hollow where the boulders lie hidden. There is an ◆ orange circuit and recently cleaned ◆ black circuit.

Mammouths

Drive into the centre of Nemours and follow signs for the *Musée de la Prehistorie*. Pass the Rimbaud school (parking for *Mont d 'Olivet*) and at the roundabout take the Poligny exit. 500m on, turn right onto an unpaved road to a car-park. Follow the GR13 up to the ridge from the *Chemin des Crottes au Loup* to a viewpoint. 200m further along the ridge you will find the bouldering on the large boulders by the path. ❐ *Ubik* is the impressive 8a undercling overhang on the north side. If this is too hard, try the excellent ❐ *Osiris* 7b on the south side, above the ledge through rounded rib holds to a long reach to the top.

❒ Coquibus > La Nuit

❒ Coquibus > Fata Morgana

❒ Coquibus Rumont > Serenity

❒ Coquibus Rumont > The Big Island

❒ Bois des Longs Vaux > Phobos Moon

❒ L'Étroit Mousse Plus Bas que Terre

Coquibus

Coquibus is a biological reserve and extremely delicate, so please do not remove vegetation, use the paths as much as possible, and in all cases leave no trace . . . brush off chalk and take litter away. There are no circuits here and the ethic is to visit single boulders with test pieces. These areas contain many superb blocs and much fun can be found hunting them down. Study your IGN map and go online for more detail before heading out.

Bois des Longs Vaux

The boulders south of the *Chemin des Grands Longs Vaux*, across the fields from the Milly bypass. Just south of the north roundabout take a NE turn onto a track in the fields (electric tower). Strike across the fields on the right road (not tower road) into the forest to parking. Take the path east into the forest, the first main boulder is visible on the right after 200m, ❒ *Phobos Moon*, a 7c jump from underclings without using the arête. Beside this is the short 7a roof SS: ❒ *Les Assis*. For the much sought after ❒ *Fata Morgana* (8a), continue further east and veer off right to the high ridge 50m before the ruined wall by the main path. Direct uphill right from the old wall is ❒ *La Nuit*, an amazing 7c roof on top of the ridge.

Coquibus Rumont

This area lies just north of the D837 Milly to Fontainebleau road behind the old Coquibus Auberge. For the Rumont boulders, park at the round car-park on the north side of the road east of Milly in the woods (red and white posts *La Boulignère*). Follow the *Chemin Boulignère* north to a second path on the right after 500m or so, follow this east for 50m and head uphill on a rough track just after a stone. 300m uphill on the right is the superb front lip roof ❒ *Serenity*, a long 7b, found on the huge roofed boulder. The SS roof direct on right is ❒ *The Big Island* – a gobsmacking 8c.

Coquibus Grandes Vallées

Further east again, park carefully in a small north-side layby by a telegraph pole at the road junction for the Musardière campsite road. Head directly into the woods to a lateral path, cross this and find some low rocks, continue uphill to find a cluster of good boulders near the hilltop. The excellent east-facing ochre wall of the lowest boulder has the excellent left jump-start sloper problem of ❒ *Délit de Sale Nom*, a hard 7a with a 7c sit start. The obvious right hand deep cave roof at the top of the hill is ❒ *L'Étroit Mousse Plus Bas que Terre*, a 7b – start as deep as possible and finish right, finishing left is 7a.

Coquibus Auvergne

Park at *La Feuillaredière* before the bridge, cross road and head along the *Chemin de la Mare d' Auvergne*. ❒ *Aurellien* is a 6a+ prow to the north of the path as it turns right. ❒ *Rebelle* is a large 7b slab left of overlap and to the east of the path on the southern hill flank over the road and houses, ❒ *King Cobra* is a large 7b+ roof on the far north-east hilltop.

Coquibus Access

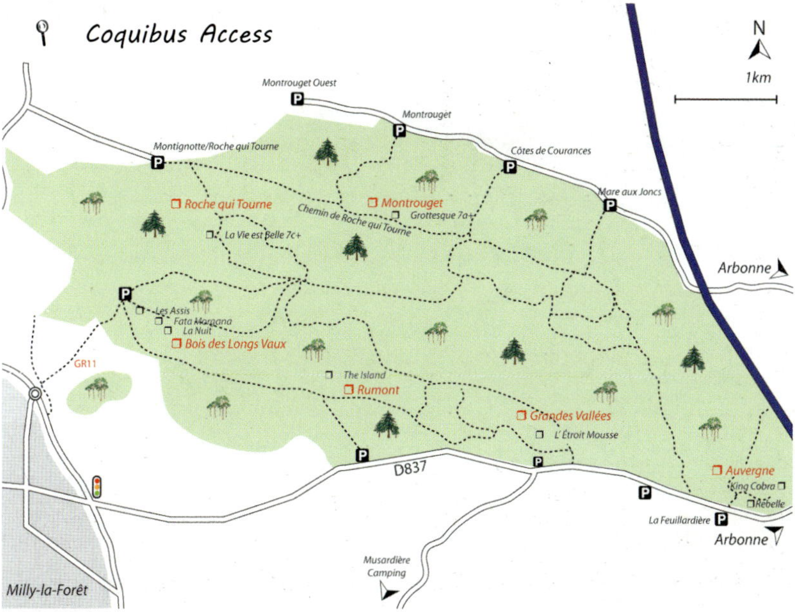

❐ Cuvier Rempart > Noir Désir > Photo © Dan Varian

Apremont > Fil a Tordre > Photo © www.morozzo.co.uk

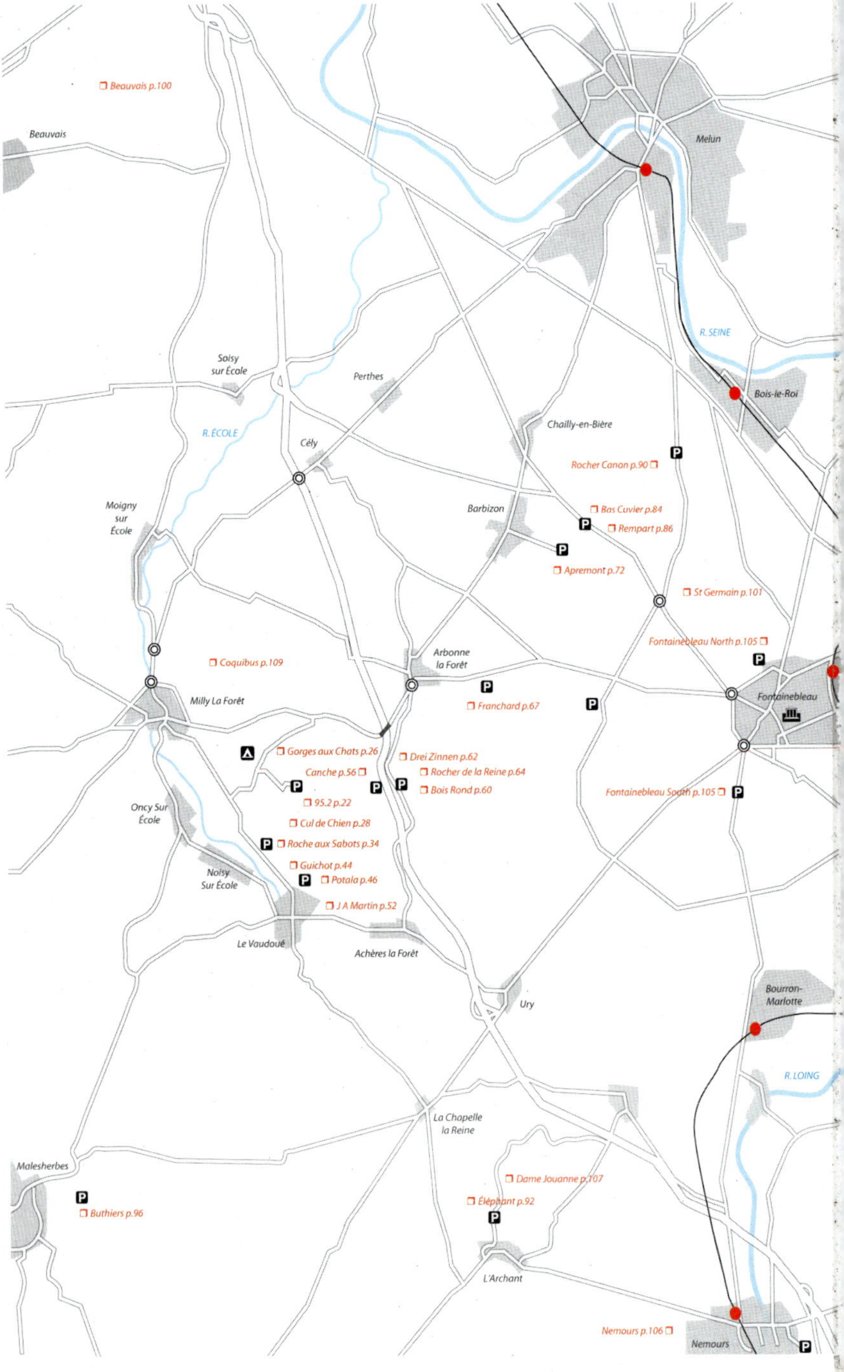
Beauvais p.100
Beauvais
Melun
R. SEINE
Bois-le-Roi
Soisy sur École
Perthes
R. ÉCOLE
Cély
Chailly-en-Bière
Rocher Canon p.90
Moigny sur École
Barbizon
Bas Cuvier p.84
Rempart p.86
Apremont p.72
St Germain p.101
Fontainebleau North p.105
Arbonne la Forêt
Coquibus p.109
Milly La Forêt
Franchard p.67
Fontainebleau
Gorges aux Chats p.26
Drei Zinnen p.62
Canche p.56
Rocher de la Reine p.64
Bois Rond p.60
Fontainebleau South p.105
95.2 p.22
Oncy Sur École
Cul de Chien p.28
Roche aux Sabots p.34
Guichot p.44
Noisy Sur École
Potala p.46
J A Martin p.52
Le Vaudoué
Achères la Forêt
Ury
Bourron-Marlotte
R. LOING
La Chapelle la Reine
Malesherbes
Dame Jouanne p.107
Éléphant p.92
Buthiers p.96
L'Archant
Nemours p.106
Nemours